United States
Department of
Agriculture

Forest Service

Pacific Northwest
Research Station

General Technical Report
PNW-GTR-780

December 2008

SnagPRO: Snag and Tree Sampling and Analysis Methods for Wildlife

Lisa J. Bate, Michael J. Wisdom, Edward O. Garton, and Shawn C. Clabough

Authors

Lisa J. Bate is a consultant research wildlife biologist, 389 LaBrant Road, Kalispell, MT 59901; **Michael J. Wisdom** is a research wildlife biologist, U.S. Department of Agriculture, Forest Service, Pacific Northwest Research Station, Forestry and Range Sciences Laboratory, 1401 Gekeler Lane, La Grande, OR 97850; **Edward O. Garton** is a professor, Fish and Wildlife Resources Department, University of Idaho, Moscow, ID 83844; **Shawn C. Clabough** is a software and Web developer, 686 Fairview Drive, Moscow, ID 83843.

Cover

Clockwise from upper left, pileated woodpecker (Evelyn Bull), researchers monitoring nest in aspen tree (Lisa Bate), large old-growth snag with nesting and roosting cavities (Evelyn Bull), and white-headed woodpecker (Lisa Bate).

Abstract

Bate, Lisa J.; Wisdom, Michael J.; Garton, Edward O.; Clabough, Shawn C. 2008. SnagPRO: snag and tree sampling and analysis methods for wildlife. Gen. Tech. Rep. PNW-GTR-780. Portland, OR: U.S. Department of Agriculture, Forest Service, Pacific Northwest Research Station. 80 p.

We describe sampling methods and provide software to accurately and efficiently estimate snag and tree densities at desired scales to meet a variety of research and management objectives. The methods optimize sampling effort by choosing a plot size appropriate for the specified forest conditions and sampling goals. Plot selection and data analyses are supported by SnagPRO, a software program designed specifically to serve our sampling methods.

We present two sampling methods to estimate density and associated characteristics of snags and trees. The first method requires sampling until a desired precision is obtained for a density estimate. The second method compares estimated densities with target densities, such as target snag densities specified under a land management plan.

Our methods of snag and tree sampling are compatible with recently developed methods of log sampling, thereby improving efficiencies by enabling the simultaneous collection of all three habitat components—snags, large trees, and logs—to meet research or management objectives for a variety of resource disciplines, including wildlife, silviculture, fuels, and soils. Recently developed methods of log sampling also use SnagPRO for data collection and analysis.

Our methods and software are particularly relevant to forest management, given that nearly all federal land use plans require monitoring of snag and tree densities in relation to management direction for wildlife. Staffing and budgets available to estimate snag and tree densities, however, are extremely limited, and thus require efficient methods to achieve acceptable accuracy. Our methods are an efficient approach for estimating snag and tree densities, particularly when combined with use of the supporting SnagPRO software.

Keywords: Cavity nester, density, foraging, large tree, nesting, monitoring, sampling technique, snags, SnagPRO, wildlife management, wildlife use, woodpecker.

Contents

Introduction

The ecological roles and importance of dead and dying wood in forest ecosystems have been the subject of increasing interest and awareness over the past decades. For many vertebrate species, standing dead trees (snags) provide essential habitat in the form of cover and food. Snags with internal pockets of decay provide insulated and protected nest, roost, or den sites (Bull and others 1997, Laudenslayer 2002, Mellen and others 2006, Rose and others 2001). Other types of snags, colonized by invertebrates, provide a rich foraging resource (Bate 1995, Bull and Holthausen 1993).

Living trees with decay also provide nest, roost, and den sites (Bull and others 1997). In Oregon, for example, Rose and others (2001) documented a myriad of wildlife species associated with tree cavities (51 species), with decayed portions of trees (45 species), with hollow trees (28 species), with bark crevices of trees (21 species), and with mistletoe clumps found in large trees (18 species). In addition, large, mature trees provide an essential foraging resource for wildlife in forest ecosystems. White-headed woodpeckers (*Picoides albolarvatus*) and other wildlife species depend on the seeds produced by mature ponderosa pines (*Pinus ponderosa* Dougl. ex Laws.) for spring and autumn foraging (Dixon 1995, Ligon 1973). As certain tree species age, they develop deep furrows that harbor increased arthropod densities for foraging birds (Bull and others 1986, Mariani and Manuwal 1990). Live trees with internal pockets of decay may be colonized by ants (for example, *Formica* spp.), which serve as a key food for several vertebrate species (Bull and others 1997). Finally, large trees are the pool for recruitment of future snags.

As primary cavity-nesters, the role of woodpeckers is integral to healthy forest ecosystems because these species excavate cavities in decayed portions of snags or live trees for nest and roost sites. These cavities are subsequently used by secondary cavity-nesting or nonexcavating vertebrates. Because of their role in providing cavities needed by many other vertebrates, woodpeckers often are considered **indicator species** (Brown 1985, Thomas and others 1979). That is, if the needs of woodpeckers are met, then the needs of the larger set of species that depend on the snags and live trees that woodpeckers modify also are met (Rose and others 2001).

Although most federal land use agencies have adopted retention and recruitment standards to maintain adequate densities of snags and large trees for wildlife, these structures have declined in abundance for various reasons (Hann and others 1997). Snags are systematically removed because of their commercial and firewood values (Bate and others 2007, Wisdom and Bate 2008) and to reduce estimated risks associated with safety, fire, and disease (Dickson and others 1983, Ffolliot 1983,

For many vertebrate species, standing dead trees (snags) provide essential habitat in the form of cover and food. Living trees with decay also provide nest, roost, and den sites.

Hann and others 1997, Styskel 1983). Large trees also are targeted for removal during timber harvest as well as for firewood. Both snags and dying trees are routinely removed during salvage-logging operations (Saab and Dudley 1998). In addition, snag retention programs on national forests are hampered by problems with safety, funds, and inconsistent standards and guidelines (Hope and McComb 1994). Consequently, the density, size, and condition of snags on national forests often do not meet management standards (Bate 1995, Morrison and others 1986).

Reduced snag densities affect more than the species that depend on snags for survival. In addition, the commodity value of timber may be diminished. Most cavity-nesters are insectivores, and are instrumental in preventing or retarding insect outbreaks (Beebe 1974, Otvos 1979). Some species of woodpeckers are known to aggregate in areas of insect outbreaks, helping to accelerate the decline of the insect populations (Otvos 1979). Foraging woodpeckers chip and probe at the bark of beetle-infested trees, altering the microenvironment of any eggs and larvae and increasing beetle susceptibility to mortality from parasites and extreme temperature fluctuations. Thomas and others (1979) provided compelling arguments and evidence in support of maintaining viable populations of woodpeckers and other insectivores to benefit forest-based economies.

Managing densities of snags and large trees is essential for ensuring that the needs of cavity-nesting and decay-dependent species are met. Recognizing the integral role of woodpeckers in forest ecosystems, Thomas and others (1979) and Brown (1985) provided some of the first guidelines for managing snag densities for woodpeckers and other snag-dependent wildlife. These guidelines, however, focused only on the nesting needs of woodpeckers. Since then, new studies indicate that more snags are required than recommended in either of these publications to provide for all needs of snag-dependent species (Bull and others 1997, Mellen and others 2006, Rose and others 2001). In Oregon, for example, at least 93 vertebrate species use snags for nesting, roosting, denning, feeding, or related life functions (Rose and others 2001). In addition, foraging structures differ from nesting and roosting structures for woodpeckers (Bate 1995, Bull and Holthausen 1993, Caton 1996, Dixon 1995), and some secondary cavity nesters, such as bats (Betts 1998, Campbell and others 1996, Ormsbee and McComb 1998) and Vaux's swifts (Bull and others 1997), use hollow trees or snags for nesting and roosting.

Monitoring snags and large trees can be inherently difficult because their densities and distributions differ extensively, as do forest conditions that hamper sampling, such as topography, seral stage, and sampling visibility.

Monitoring snags and large trees can be inherently difficult because their densities and distributions differ extensively, as do forest conditions that hamper sampling, such as topography, seral stage, and sampling visibility (Bate and others 2007, Wisdom and Bate 2008). Therefore, to improve the efficiency of snag and large-tree monitoring programs, resource specialists must first determine the shape and size of plot that works best in a given area. Bull and others (1990) tested the efficiency and accuracy of both fixed- and variable-radius circular plots to determine snag densities. They found that 1-acre (0.4-ha) fixed and variable plots, with a factor-5 prism, worked best for areas with snag densities ranging from 0.7 to 2 snags per acre (1.7 to 4.9 snags/ha). Although large circular plots may be adequate for sampling open forests with relatively low snag densities, it is not possible to accurately count snags with plots of this size and shape in areas obscured by vegetation or in steep terrain (Bate and others 1999). In addition, where snag densities are high, such as in beetle-killed or burned areas, the use of large, circular plots will increase sample variance, making it difficult to obtain a precise estimate (Bate and others 1999).

Prisms or gauges can also be used to sample snags or trees along a transect line, referred to as horizontal line sampling (Husch and others 1972). Ducey and others (2002) presented a modification of horizontal line sampling (MHLS) that uses shorter segments and then adds one-half of a conventional horizontal point sample at the end of each line. Ducey and others (2002) found the modified line sampling to be more efficient and precise than traditional line sampling. As with variable-radius circular plots, however, a small prism usually is required to obtain adequate samples when snags are rare. This poses a substantial bias, however, of being unable to detect snags often hidden at the longer distances required by the sampling method, resulting in underestimation of snag densities (Harmon and Sexton 1996).

Kenning and others (2005) investigated the efficiency and bias of various snag inventory methods including fixed circular plots (1/20th acre [0.02 ha]), MHLS (Ducey and others 2002), N-tree distance sampling, and distance-limited N-tree sampling. The N-tree sampling method measures snag characteristics on a specified number of snags (N) from a center point. Under N-tree distance sampling, the maximum sampling distance was unlimited. In distance-limited N-tree sampling, the maximum sampling distance was 8 m. Kenning and others (2005) tested N-tree sampling with N = 1, N = 2, and N = 3. They found that small, fixed-area plots were most efficient for estimating density and that MHLS was best for estimating basal area.

Bütler and Schlaepfer (2004) tested a new method of quantifying large snags by coupling color infrared aerial photographs and a geographical information system (GIS) in spruce forests of Switzerland. They were encouraged by their results for large snags in these forest conditions, but did observe different degrees of accuracy based on tree diameter, treetop condition (intact or broken), and canopy closure. Other factors such as aspect, surface slope, weather, and hour of flight also affected the snag detection rate. Consequently, Bütler and Schlaepfer (2004) suggested

Although large circular plots may be adequate for sampling open forests with relatively low snag densities, it is not possible to accurately count snags with plots of this size and shape in areas obscured by vegetation or in steep terrain.

further testing to obtain the appropriate coefficient to correct for underestimation of snag densities when using this method.

As Krebs (1989) documented, most ecologists have found that rectangular or other long, thin plots are more accurate and efficient than circular or square plots. Forest habitat components are never uniformly distributed, and clumps or patches of habitat, such as snags and trees, are common. Rectangular plots are better for sampling because they cross more clumps of snags or trees, rather than either encircling or missing them completely. Consequently, use of rectangular or other long, thin plots results in lower sample variance, which translates into smaller sample sizes required to obtain desired precision.

Whereas rectangular plots are recognized as the optimal plot **shape** for sampling in patchy or clumped habitats (Krebs 1989), the optimal plot size differs among forest types depending on the abundance and distribution of the snag or tree size of interest. The determination of optimal plot size is affected by a variety of conditions and objectives, all of which can be efficiently and accurately considered with the use of SnagPRO. The SnagPRO program was designed not only to identify optimal plot size, but to help users design field surveys, to guide and facilitate data collection with use of standard, electronic field forms, to estimate required sample sizes needed to achieve desired precision, and to analyze all results in ways that are statistically valid and that meet sampling objectives. SnagPRO provides practical tutorials with sample data sets to demonstrate use of the software in survey design, field sampling, and data analysis.

In the following sections, we describe our sampling methods and provide examples with SnagPRO to design surveys, conduct sampling, and analyze data for estimating snag and tree densities at desired scales. We provide example tutorials and address all aspects of the estimation process.

General Information

Downloading and Installing SnagPRO

Download SnagPRO (version 1.0) from the USDA Forest Service Pacific Northwest (PNW) Web site at http://www.fs.fed.us/pnw/publications/tools-databases.shtml. SnagPRO installation requires at least 5 MB of space. SnagPRO requires another 10 to 50 MB of space to operate. Users may choose where to install SnagPRO; the default location is C:\Program Files. Once installed, users may create a shortcut to SnagPRO for their desktops or Quick Launch bar.

There will be a Microsoft Excel file—Snag_Tutorial_Data.xls—accompanying the zipped SnagPRO file that needs to be downloaded. This file contains four worksheets. Two contain sample snag data sets for use with the tutorials found at

---

SnagPRO was designed to identify optimal plot size, help design field surveys, facilitate data collection with electronic field forms, estimate sample sizes, and analyze results.

the end of this report. One worksheet contains a sample data form for printing and hard-copy use in the field. The fourth worksheet is for users who want to enter their data directly into a spreadsheet file while in the field. Other electronic formats can be used in the field but then need to be formatted as shown in the examples below before importing to SnagPRO for analysis.

User's existing resource data—from spreadsheet or database—must be correctly formatted as a comma-separated value (CSV) file before importing to Snag-PRO. For simplicity, this report addresses only spreadsheet examples, and data files for the tutorial are in spreadsheet format.

Sampling Applications

Our sampling methods can be used to gain knowledge about snag or tree habitats for any wildlife species of interest. For example, knowledge of the difference in large (≥16 in [40 cm] diameter at breast height [d.b.h.]) wildlife tree densities between two foraging areas for brown creeper (*Certhia americana*) or red tree voles (*Arborimus longicaudus*) may be of interest. Similarly, a land use plan may call for monitoring snag and wildlife tree densities for white-headed woodpecker in a landscape dominated by intensive timber production versus another landscape dominated by wilderness designation. Or, mitigation of timber harvest practices may call for retention of snags >20 in (5.1 cm) d.b.h. that are likely to serve as nest structures for pileated woodpeckers (*Dryocopus pileatus*).

Our methods also are appropriate for other resource disciplines needing statistically valid estimates of snag and tree densities. Plot sizes can be adjusted easily to accommodate small-diameter (for example, saplings) or large-diameter snags or large trees as necessary for different resource objectives. The methods may also complement the data collected in other projects (for example, project planning, effects analyses, stand exam or Forest Inventory and Analysis [FIA] data) by converting data to similar units of measurement (for example, number/acre [number/ha]) to provide additional baseline comparisons for resource planning and management.

Our sampling methods can be used to gain knowledge about snag or tree habitats for any wildlife species of interest and are appropriate for other resource disciplines needing statistically valid esitmates of snag and tree densities.

Methods

General Snag and Large-Tree Sampling Guidelines

A condensed outline of the guidelines for sampling snags and trees can be found in appendix 1. A more detailed discussion of topics in the outline follows.

Sampling Objectives (Step 1)

Most ecological studies are designed to answer some form of the question: How many are there? For example, do harvested areas comply with snag density standards of the land management plan? How many large trees are available for future snag recruitment? Or, how many large snags suitable for nesting Lewis' woodpeckers (*Melanerpes lewis*) are available in a burned area? Therefore, the first step in any sampling program is to specify the sampling objective(s). The objectives ultimately determine the amount of time and resources needed to obtain estimates at a desired precision. Answering the following questions will help determine the objectives:

1. What snag (tree) size(s) will be surveyed (diameter and height)?
2. How will data be used? For land use allocation? For compliance monitoring? Or to respond to land use appeals or other legal actions? The purpose often dictates answers to the following questions.
3. How precise does the estimate need to be?
4. Is snag/tree species important? If so, why?
5. Will signs of wildlife use be recorded (for example, woodpecker foraging, nest, or roost cavities)?
6. Are estimates for separate areas needed?

> **Time spent on extraneous data collection limits sample size and the subsequent results.**

As Krebs (1989) stated, "Not everything that can be measured should be." It is common to collect information on everything possible while in the field. Yet, the time spent on extraneous data collection limits sample size and the subsequent results. For example, examining each snag for cavities may seem like a simple addition to the field protocol. Yet, the time spent examining a tall snag on all sides for cavities can substantially increase the amount of time spent surveying a given transect length, especially for inexperienced field crews. Therefore, it is important to establish clear objectives and explicitly describe how data will be used before starting fieldwork.

Regarding precision levels for most sampling activities, we recommend a design to obtain estimates within 20 percent of the true mean 90 percent of the time. We have set these values as defaults in SnagPRO. Sampling to achieve a higher precision (for example, within 10 percent of the true mean 95 percent of the time) would be cost and area prohibitive for habitat components that are relatively rare and have clumped distributions. Only when habitat components are relatively abundant and randomly distributed would higher precision be manageable.

Landscape Definition and Selection (Step 2)

The second step is to define the landscape, or area of interest, by delineating the boundaries. This area is the sampling frame, within which a random sample is drawn for the purpose of making inferences to the entire area. Our sampling methods are designed to be compatible with the snag and large-tree sampling methods previously developed by Bate and others (1999). These methods were based on a sampling unit defined as a landscape (sampling frame) ranging from about 3,000 to 6,900 acres or 1200 to 2800 hectares (Bull and others 1991). These sampling methods can also be used on a subwatershed scale with a few modifications. See "Establishing Transects" and "Compare to Target" sections for details. Subwatersheds within the Columbia River Basin region can be as large as 20,000 acres, or 8100 hectares (Quigley and others 1996).

The sample area need not be a delineated subwatershed, but may be a smaller area like a research natural area including less than 1,000 acres (400 ha). Whether these sampling methods can be used within even smaller areas (<100 acres [40 ha]) depends on the density and distribution of snags and trees in the sizes of interest. Burned habitats will likely have enough snags to make these sampling procedures practical with small plot sizes. To obtain a density estimate of large (>20-in [51-cm] d.b.h.) snags in an unburned forest of the same area, a complete count may be more appropriate.

Landscape Stratification (Step 3)

Perhaps the most critical step in snag or tree sampling is the stratification process. Although the initial investment of time spent in the stratification process may seem large, if done correctly, it should reduce the final requirement of resources and provide a more precise estimate (Krebs 1989). Existing stratifications, such as those used by silviculturists to conduct stand exams, can be readily adapted for stratifications used to sample snags and trees. If snag and tree sampling is to occur simultaneously with log sampling, stratification designs based on snag abundance are appropriate because obtaining precise estimates of snags is often more difficult than for trees or logs, owing to the low abundance and patchy distribution of snags.

Whether to stratify a landscape before sampling depends on several factors. Cochran (1977) identified the three most common reasons.

- Stratification may produce a gain in precision of the estimate. If the landscape is heterogeneous (highly variable) in abundance of snags or trees, establishing individual strata that are homogeneous (same) within each stratum can substantially improve precision.

- Sampling problems can differ for parts of the landscape with different forest community types, timber harvest methods, and seral stages; stratifying by these conditions will allow appropriate sample size allocation among these different conditions, again increasing precision.

- Separate estimates are desired for certain subdivisions of the landscape. For example, part of a subwatershed may be managed for timber production,

Stratification should reduce the final requirement of resources and provide a more precise estimate.

another managed as a research natural area, and a third managed as a wilderness area.

If one or more of the above reasons are relevant, it is beneficial to stratify. SnagPRO can accommodate up to four strata. We set the limit at four strata because it is rare that more than four sampling categories will be used. In particular, with increasing number of strata comes the law of diminishing returns. That is, for each additional stratum, there needs to be an additional 10 transects (400 ft or 100 m) of sampling line. If, however, resource specialists find that they need to divide a landscape into five or more strata, they can use the **Simple-Random Sampling Equation** page within SnagPRO to obtain their stratum means (equation 2) and variances (equation 9) and then calculate a stratified mean estimate and its bound using equations 12 through 14. If the landscape is homogeneous throughout in regard to snag and tree densities, there is probably little to be gained from stratification.

Use the following steps to stratify your survey area:

1. Visit the area to identify areas with general differences in snag and tree densities, vegetation types, and structural conditions. These differences should be noted and marked on the map.

2. Following the initial field visit, obtain more accurate reference maps for field use, such as GIS maps, U.S. Geological Survey (USGS) orthoquad maps, or both. Make sure that appropriate metadata (data definitions) are included for all GIS layers or maps to be used. Maps should include the following information:

   a. Road system, road types, and maintenance level of roads.

   b. Polygon or vegetation units and their respective unique numeric identifiers.

   c. Current seral stage of vegetation at a scale of 1:31,680, or better resolution. Keep in mind that scale is a ratio or fraction, so polygons mapped at 1:24,000-scale will appear larger than they do in the 1:31,680-scale map. This information may be on one or more maps.

3. Query the polygon database for detailed information about each polygon such as forest type (low versus high elevation, dry versus moist), management history, seral stage, disturbance history (wind, fire, insects, and disease), and any other factors that may affect snag/tree abundance. The output of your query will be a simple report of polygon data attributes. Ensure that the report includes types of management activities, such as harvest method used, slash and burn prescriptions, thinning, and snag and tree retention standards that potentially apply to each area or land use allocation.

4. Ground check the map and polygon data using aerial photographs. Generally, the amount of time that must be spent to stratify the polygons in the field is inversely proportional to the quality of the GIS layers available. Carefully review the metadata and discuss any concerns with the GIS specialist to ensure that characteristics of the spatial data, particularly its accuracy and how it was collected or derived, are well understood.

5. Revisit the survey area with the field maps. Plan to spend at least one day to validate the information on the map(s) and in the report from the database query.

6. Assign each polygon to a stratum. Estimate the number of acres (ha) within each polygon or stratum.

Most landscapes surveyed for snags/trees have undergone some amount of timber harvest. Consequently, depending on the method of timber harvest, the placement of each polygon within a stratum may or may not be straightforward. For example, if snags are of interest, most unharvested mature/old-growth stands in mixed-conifer forests support a high abundance of snags. By contrast, older harvest units that have been clearcut may have few snags. Finally, more recent clearcut units may have snags distributed throughout the polygon, reflecting more recent policy changes.

For these conditions, combine all unharvested mature/old-growth stands into a single stratum. Then determine the time period when snag retention began in timber harvest units, and ground check some example units. Combine these stands into a stratum. Finally, combine all older harvest units into another stratum. Generate a new map of all stands categorized as one of three strata: (1) stands that were clearcut before adoption of snag retention standards, (2) stands that were clearcut since adoption of snag retention standards, and (3) unharvested mature/old-growth stands.

Further designating the individual strata is more time-consuming for areas where selection harvest has occurred, especially if GIS stand data are unavailable. In this situation, use ocular stratification by tree composition and varying snag densities. For example, in a subwatershed composed of a mix of ponderosa pine and lodgepole pine (*Pinus contorta* Dougl. ex Loud.) stands, three strata might be possible: (1) stands dominated by ponderosa pine with few snags observed; (2) stands represented by co-dominance of ponderosa and lodgepole pine trees, usually with 1 or 2 snags per acre observed; and (3) stands dominated by lodgepole pine with 5 or more snags per acre observed.

The primary criterion in stratifying a subwatershed is the **sampling objective**. If sampling is intended to estimate the density of large trees only, stratification is dictated solely by this variable. If both large trees and snags will be sampled, base the stratification on which structure varies most in abundance. The secondary criterion is either **seral stage** or **timber harvest technique**, which affect not only precision but also the level of sampling difficulty during fieldwork. The tertiary criterion is **forest community type**, especially for stands affected by insect- or disease-based mortality events. Certain tree species are more susceptible to insects or diseases, and these stands will have higher densities of snags, such as mixed stands of lodgepole and ponderosa pine. Finally, consider **land management use**. Do you need separate estimates for areas that are managed for different purposes (for example, riparian versus timber production areas)?

Establishing Transects (Step 4)

Conducting a pilot survey is one of the most important steps of any snag or tree survey. In a pilot survey, there are two primary objectives:

- Collect preliminary data by which to identify the optimal plot size.
- Obtain an estimate of the total number of samples required to meet a user's objectives.

Pilot data are not extraneous data to be discarded. Rather, they are the first samples collected, and are included in the variable estimates for the entire sampling area. In areas where snags or trees in the targeted size classes are abundant, the pilot survey may provide an adequate number of samples to meet a user's objectives. By contrast, in areas where snag or tree abundance is low, analyzing the pilot data to determine the optimal plot size can minimize the number of samples needed to achieve the desired precision. Use the optimal plot size to collect the remainder of the data.

We designed the transects for snag and tree sampling to be compatible with transects used for log sampling, thus improving the efficiency of the fieldwork.

We designed the transects for snag and tree sampling to be compatible with transects used for log sampling (Bate and others 2008), thus improving the efficiency of the fieldwork by allowing all three structural components to be sampled simultaneously. The original snag and large-tree sampling protocol recommended 800 ft (200 m) within each stand on stratified landscapes (Bate and others 1999); however, instead of using the single 800-ft (200-m) transect, split it into two 400-ft (100-m)-long sections called transects. These two smaller transects capture more of the variability occurring in a single stand and increase compatibility with log sampling (Bate and others 2008). Subdivide each transect into smaller increments, called subsegments, and sample for the three habitat components of snags, large trees, and logs. This standardizes the sampling protocol and allows SnagPRO to determine the optimal transect length for each variable in relation to the specific forest conditions.

Two options exist for establishing transects: the single-stratum landscape method and the stratified method. For the single-stratum landscape method, follow these steps to establish transects within a single stand or a nonstratified landscape:

1. Randomly place a grid over the area.
2. Randomly select 10 grid points for sampling.
3. Randomly select compass bearings for each of the 10 transect starting points.

For the stratified method on heterogeneous landscapes composed of numerous stands or units, it may be more efficient to randomly select stands for sampling. To do this:

1. Select stands for sampling by randomly picking stand unit numbers from the complete list of stands within that stratum.
2. Place a grid over the stand.
3. Randomly pick two grid points within each stand.
4. Randomly pick compass bearings for each point.

Use a random number generator or random numbers table for either method, or generate random numbers for compass bearings using the second hand of a watch. If a watch is used to generate random starting direction, multiply the number of seconds (60) by six to obtain numbers from 6 to 360 that can be used as compass bearings for the starting point.

The pilot survey should include:

- A minimum of two transects per stand (fig. 1) to adequately represent the variability in each stand and stratum, providing a better estimate of the sample size required to meet objectives.
- A total of at least eight 400-ft-long transects (English users), or ten 100-m-long transects (metric users), within each stratum.

When establishing transects, it is important to realize that the equations used in SnagPRO assume a normal distribution (Krebs 1989). However, snags are rarely normally distributed, instead occurring in clumps. Therefore, a minimum of 60 samples is usually needed to achieve a normal distribution. Users should consult with a statistician if they are unsure as to whether their data are normally distributed in relation to the number of samples. Avoid overlapping the transects because the equations assume that no snags or trees are sampled more than once.

For larger subwatersheds, the stands in the pilot survey should not be close together, especially for subwatersheds encompassing several plant communities.

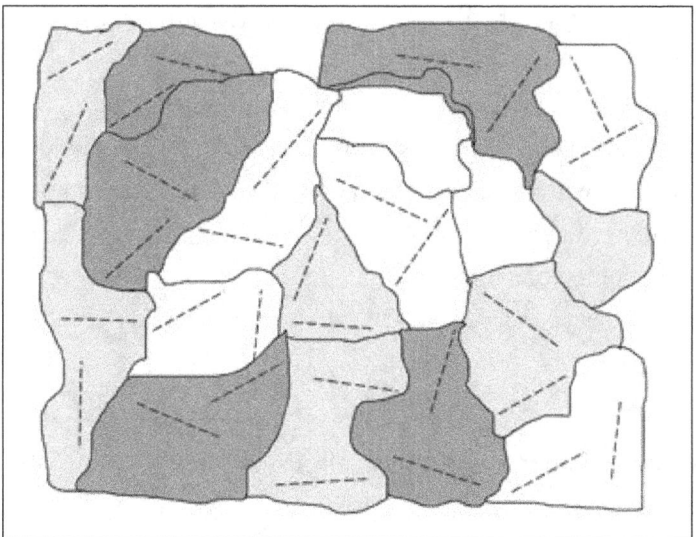

Figure 1—Illustration of transect establishment for snag or large-tree pilot survey on a landscape with three strata. Five stands within each stratum should be selected. Within each stand, two 100-m or 400-ft transects are established. Each transect within the entire landscape is given a unique numeric identifier and is divided into eight 12.5-m or 50-ft-long subsegments. Subsegments are numbered from 1 to 8 on each transect.

In this situation, divide the subwatershed into three sections and equally divide the samples throughout the sections.

Field Techniques (Step 5)

Fieldwork requires some or all of the field equipment listed in table 1. Where shrub cover is thick, the 100- or 200-ft (English users) or 50-m (metric users) fiberglass surveyor's tape (with a logger's nail taped to one end) is very efficient for marking the center transect line. One person walks the centerline, locating targeted size classes of snags or trees, and taking all measurements. The second person ensures quality control and records data on field forms.

Quality control is best accomplished by having the data recorder walk some distance away from the centerline. This ensures that all snags on the centerline are counted (surprisingly, snags on the centerline are the ones most likely to be missed because observers look mainly to the side). The data recorder also helps ensure that the tape is held perpendicular to the centerline when measuring the distance of a snag or tree from the line. Relascopes may also be used to gauge the distance of a snag or tree from the transect line. However, a relascope estimates the distance from the closest edge of a snag or tree and not to its central axis. Therefore, measuring the actual distance with a logger's tape is needed for all borderline cases.

Quality control is best accomplished by having the data recorder walk some distance away from the centerline.

Table 1—Field equipment for snag and tree sampling

Item	Use
Accurate map of polygon units or vegetation cover types	Record correct stratum number
Road map	Determine location and access
Aerial photographs	Determine stratum and locations
Orthophoto quads	Determine stratum and locations
Field data forms (hard or electronic)	Record survey information
Engineer's surveyor tape (50 m or 100 or 200 ft long)	Measure transect distances; mark centerline
Logger's tape	Measure distance of snag or tree from transect or required distance away for heights
Calipers	Measure diameter of snags or trees
Relascope	Measure distance of snag or tree from transect or required distance away for heights
Compass	Determine bearings
Pocket knife	Determine species and decay class of snags
Flagging	Mark ends of subsegments, if necessary

SnagPRO's standardized field forms include the snag or tree information needed for all analyses. Field forms can be customized for each location and survey. For simultaneous collection of data on snags, trees, and logs, data are recorded in separate files for each component.

We found that hand-held computers are useful for fieldwork, and SnagPRO is designed accordingly. Users can avoid entering data twice by using the Data_entry worksheet to enter data directly on a hand-held computer while sampling in the field. The Date_entry worksheet is found in the Snag_Tutorial_Data.xls file. If hand-held computers are not used for fieldwork, create hardcopy field forms from the worksheet labeled "Field form" found within the Snag_Tutorial_Data.xls file. Open the Snag_Tutorial_Data.xls file, highlight the entire page that has gridlines, and choose **Selection**, instead of Sheet, under the Print options for a hardcopy form with gridlines.

Appendix 2 provides a sampling protocol to collect data for snag and large-tree habitat. Copy this appendix to a new file and customize it for your fieldwork. Customizing options include:

- Defining a qualifying snag or tree by diameter and height.
- Using either numeric or four- to six-letter alpha codes for snag and tree species.
- Altering data requirements for each variable to meet sampling objectives, such as recording heights to the nearest foot or meter.
- Defining snag decay classes or tree structural classes.
- Recording wildlife signs, if desired.

Default plot sizes—

There are four default widths available for both English (fig. 2) and metric systems (fig. 3): 33, 66, 99, and 132 ft; and 10, 20, 30, and 40 m. These widths are whole widths of the plot, measuring from one side, across the centerline, to the other side. In SnagPRO, these plot sizes in English units are labeled Width33, Width66, Width99, and Width132. For metric units, they are labeled Width10, Width20, Width30, and Width40.

The half-width is half the distance from the centerline in which you count all snags or trees, based on the chosen plot width. The half-width distance of these plots is 16.5, 33, 49.5, and 66 ft (or 5, 10, 15, and 20 m). When measuring distance, be sure to measure all snags and trees to their midpoints, or central axis.

Four default plot lengths are available: 50, 100, 200, and 400 ft (12.5, 25, 50, and 100 m). For studies that use only one transect length such as segments (100-ft or 25-m lengths), it is still necessary to assign a transect and subsegment (50-ft or 12.5-m length) number to each length and keep track of the smallest increments (subsegments). Later, users may indicate in SnagPRO that only segment lengths are desired.

Custom plot sizes—

Different sampling objectives may require different plot sizes. Remember that for optimal transect length analyses, transects should be twice as long as sections; sections twice as long as segments; and segments twice as long as subsegments. SnagPRO can also accept customized plot widths. Both customized widths and lengths are adjusted under Custom Dimensions found under the Plot Dimensions menu.

Survey—

Conduct the pilot survey to determine the optimal plot size with these steps:

1. Use an engineer's surveying or measuring tape to establish transects, starting each transect from the randomly selected points (described above).

2. Assign a unique numeric identifier to each transect, delineating the subsegment lengths (50 ft [or 12.5 m]) as you walk along the transect (400 ft or 100 m).

3. Number each transect's subsegments 1 through 8.

4. Conduct a complete count of all snags or trees of interest within 66 ft (20 m) of each side of the centerline, using the tape as centerline. A snag or tree is "in" if its midpoint is ≤66 ft (20 m), as measured perpendicularly, from the centerline.

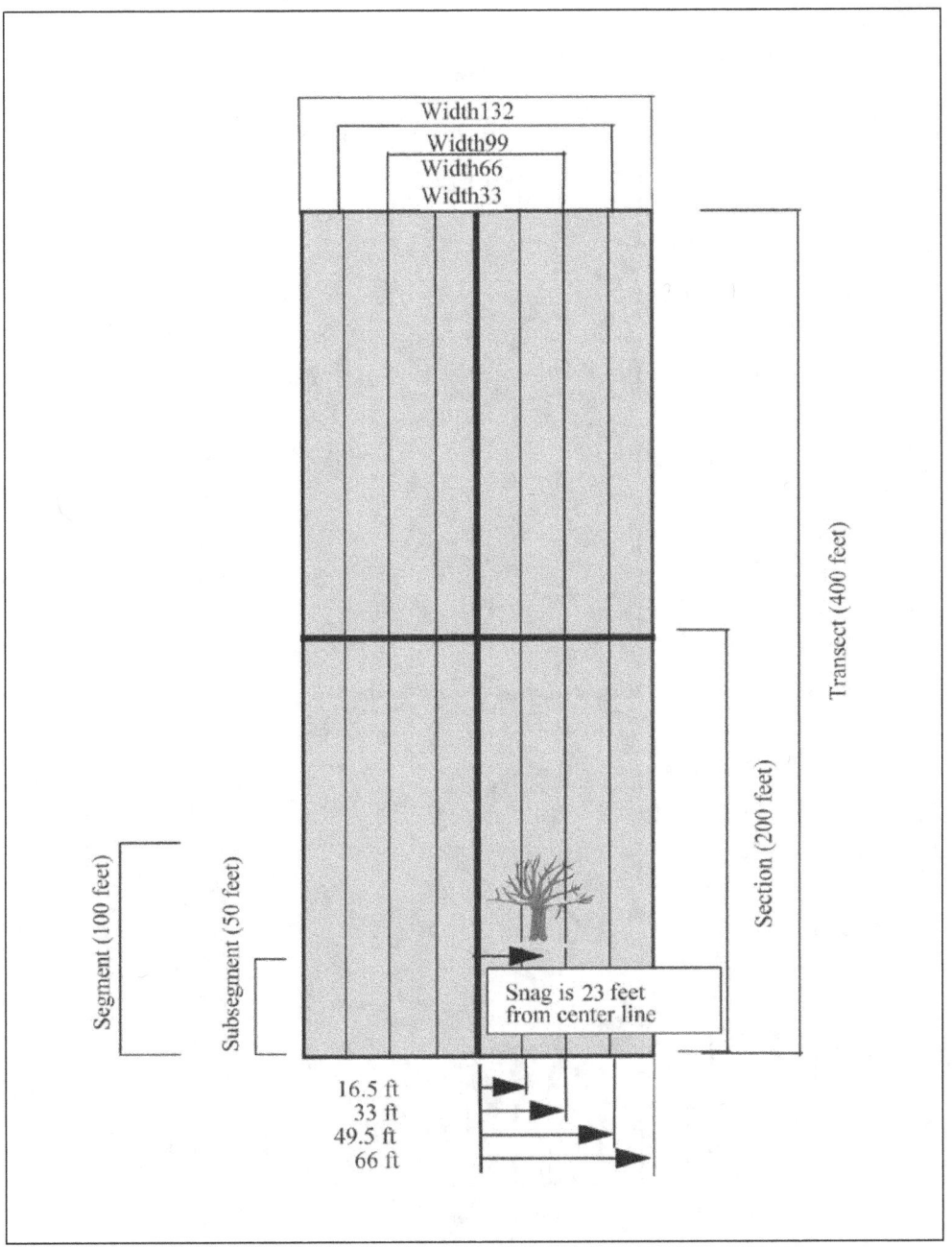

Figure 2—There are 16 default plot sizes available using the English measurement system. During the pilot survey, the distance of all qualifying snags or trees is measured in the maximum half width (66 ft). Then after the optimal plot size has been determined, this optimal plot width is used for the remainder of the survey. The Width33 to Width132 refer to the entire width of the plot (in feet). Therefore, only snags or trees whose measured distance (from centerline) is ≤ half of the entire width qualify for a specific plot size when determining the optimal plot size. For example, a snag that is 23 ft from the centerline would be counted in the Width66, Width99, and Width132 plots. It does not qualify, however, for the Width33 plot because its distance is more than 16.5 ft (the half width) from the centerline.

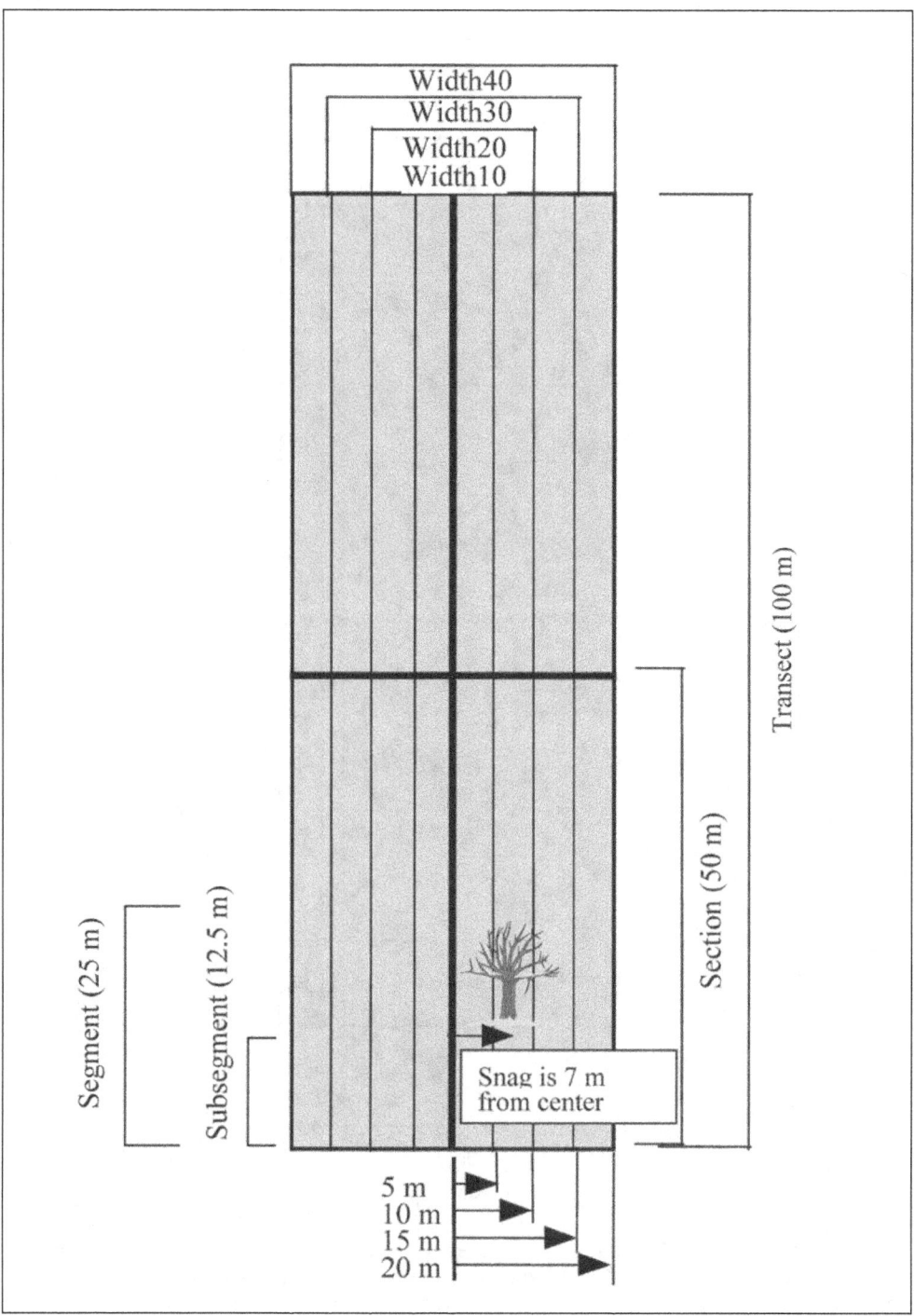

Figure 3—There are 16 default plot sizes available using the metric measurement system. During the pilot survey, the distance of all qualifying snags or trees is measured in the maximum half width (20 m). Then after the optimal plot size has been determined, this optimal plot width is used for the remainder of the survey. The Width10 to Width40 plots refer to the entire width of the plot (in meters). Therefore, only snags or trees whose measured distance (from centerline) is ≤ half of the entire width qualify for a specific plot size when determining the optimal plot size. For example, a snag that is 7 m from the centerline would be counted in the Width20, Width30, and Width40 plots. It does not qualify, however, for the Width10 plot because its distance is more than 5 m (the half width) from the centerline.

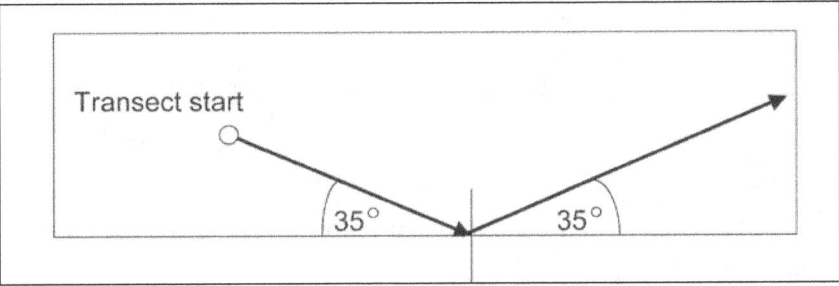

Figure 4—Illustration of randomly oriented transect hitting the edge and "bouncing" back within the sampling area. This ensures edges are included in the sampling population, while maintaining the option to analyze data for the optimal transect length.

Exceptions—

Modify the plot width when sampling visibility is ≤33 ft [10 m]) or high densities of snags or trees result in >15 snags or trees recorded in each plot. In these conditions, only count snags and trees out 33 ft (10 m) from either side of the centerline for the optimal plot size analysis. See "Presampling plot size selection" below for other exceptions.

Occasionally, the random compass bearing for a transect will cause it to continue outside the boundary of the sampling area. Use the "bounce back" method to keep the transect within the stand. The bounce-back method is similar to hitting a billiard ball or racquetball against a sidewall, and having it travel back away from the wall at the same angle. In your sample area, determine the angle at which the transect hits the edge, then use this same angle to continue (fig. 4) back into the sample area. This technique allows resource specialists to determine the optimal length and include the edges of the stand in the sampling pool.

Presampling plot size selection—

Rather than conducting the optimal plot size analysis (See Optimal Plot Size in the "SnagPRO Analysis" section), it may be more practical to preselect a plot size for sampling, based on information gathered during the stratification process. For example, in a clearcut stratum where travel is easy and snag density is low (<1 snag per acre [0.4 snag/ha]), a statistical review of the data may reveal little about the optimal plot size. In such cases, use a wider plot (132 ft or 40 m wide) to collect data efficiently on as many snags as possible. For small clumps of snags retained within harvest units, recording the distance from the centerline to each snag may be advantageous if the variability proves too great with use of the wider plots. This will enable you to use only snags in a narrower plot if deemed necessary.

In mature/old-growth forests, 20- by 50-m plots are commonly used to sample snags, especially where terrain is steep and rugged, or vegetation is dense. In these conditions, the wider plots are inefficient and prone to inaccuracies. By contrast, the narrower plots make it easier to detect snags and large trees within the plot boundaries and to measure their distances.

In areas where snag numbers tend to be low, but clumps of snags are present, the longer, narrower plots work best to minimize the variance. Burned habitats with high densities of evenly distributed snags present a different challenge. Here, the shorter plots would likely work best. This is also true for sampling live trees that are high in abundance and evenly distributed.

The advantage of preselecting a sample plot width is that the distance of each snag or tree from the centerline does not have to be recorded, saving time in the field during the pilot survey. The disadvantage is that users lose the option of determining the optimal plot width. Note that once you determine the optimal plot width, there is no need to continue measuring distances; enter a "1" in the distance column as a placeholder after a plot width is established.

SnagPRO guides users in their selection of the optimal plot size.

Postsampling selection—

For many conditions, the optimal plot size for sampling is unknown until a pilot sample provides estimates of the density and distribution of the snags or trees in the area. This is a key strength of SnagPRO in that it guides users in their selection of the optimal plot size that minimizes the sampling effort while attaining the sampling objectives. Once the plot optimal width is identified, the Optimal Plot Size option can continue to be used for analysis of optimal length, but without the need to measure the distance of each snag or tree from the centerline. See the "Optimal Plot Size" section for details.

Distribution and abundance of snags or trees influence the optimal plot size. Generally, the more abundant the habitat component of interest, the smaller the plot needed. In areas of clumped snags or trees of high abundance, narrower plots are the better choice. How narrow can be difficult to ascertain without first collecting pilot data. In the pilot survey, collect data for the length and at both the 10- and 20-m (33- and 66-ft) widths.

Data Collection

The following are mandatory fields requiring information for SnagPRO to operate correctly (fig. 5). Refer to appendix 2 for details about each field variable.

For each qualifying snag or tree (that meets the stipulated criteria) along a transect, record the following:

1. Stratum number
2. Transect number
3. Subsegment number

Stratum	Location	Transect	Subsegment	Distance	Species	Class	Dbh	Height	Cavity	Forage
1	2345	1	1	9999						
1	2345	1	2	2	2	1	64	32.6	1	3
1	2345	1	3	5	2	5	41	2.7	2	4
1	2345	1	4	13	2	2	74	26.5	1	1
1	2345	1	5	7	2	3	76	17.7	5	4
1	2345	1	6	11	2	2	69	25.9	4	3
1	2345	1	7	8	2	2	61	23.8	3	4
1	2345	1	8	9999						
1	2345	2	1	6	2	2	33	19.2	4	4
1	2345	2	2	10	2	3	46	13.7	4	2
1	2345	2	3	3	2	5	28	2.4	4	3
1	2345	2	4	11	2	5	31	9.8	4	4
1	2345	2	5	15	2	4	89	15.2	4	4
1	2345	2	6	10	2	4	41	15.2	4	4
1	2345	2	7	8	2	4	38	13.7	4	2
1	2345	2	8	0	2	3	61	14.3	2	4
1	4567	3	1	12	2	4	48	19.2	5	2
1	4567	3	2	1	2	1	94	38.1	5	4
1	4567	3	3	9	2	3	56	35.4	5	3
1	4567	3	4	2	2	5	56	2.4	5	4
1	4567	3	5	3	2	3	102	30.8	2	4
1	4567	3	6	1	2	1	94	38.1	5	4
1	4567	3	7	9999						
1	4567	3	8	10	2	1	32	26.2	4	3
1	4567	4	1	9999						
1	4567	4	2	9999						
1	4567	4	3	9999						
1	4567	4	4	9	2	4	76	29	3	3
1	4567	4	5	4	2	5	28	2.1	4	2
1	4567	4	6	16	2	2	33	12.5	4	3
1	4567	4	7	3	2	3	102	30.8	2	4
1	4567	4	8	9999						
1	6789	5	1	5	2	5	41	2.7	2	4
1	6789	5	2	9999						
1	6789	5	3	9999						
1	6789	5	4	4	2	2	33	12.5	4	3
1	6789	5	5	9999						
1	6789	5	6	12	2	3	49	30	4	4
1	6789	5	7	5	2	3	64	37.2	4	4
1	6789	5	8	9999						
1	6789	6	1	0	2	2	61	23.5	4	2
1	6789	6	2	9	2	2	64	16.2	5	2
1	6789	6	3	15	2	3	43	15.5	4	2
1	6789	6	4	9999						
1	6789	6	5	8	2	2	71	32	3	4
1	6789	6	6	6	2	1	58	32.6	4	2
1	6789	6	7	10	2	3	46	13.7	4	2
1	6789	6	8	11	2	2	48	21.3	4	1

Figure 5—Example of properly formatted data. This format is required before saving as a comma-separated, .csv file and importing to SnagPRO. Class refers to decay (snags) or structural (trees) stage.

4. Perpendicular distance of the midpoint of the snag or tree from the center-line (when using preselected widths just enter "1" as a place holder)
5. Species
6. Decay (snags) or structural (large tree) class
7. D.b.h.
8. Height (for surveys where all snags ≥6 ft (1.8 m) are recorded, record a minimum height).

Optional fields are Location, Cavity, and Forage. Location can correspond to (1) the stand number from which the transect originates, (2) the transect starting position determined by a global positioning system (GPS), or (3) the universal transverse meridian (UTM) coordinates of the transect starting point.

User-defined fields may also be recorded during surveys, but only include this data in columns to the right of those in the CSV file (fig. 5) that are needed for importing to SnagPRO. Additional habitat variables can be added, such as seral stage of the stand, distance to the nearest edge, and immediate habitat surrounding a snag or tree.

Distance is the most important variable, so take care to record it accurately. For cases where snags or trees are not encountered, record "9999" in the distance column. This is a critical step; it allows SnagPRO to distinguish plots without snags or trees from plots that have snags or trees with a distance of "0" because the structures are located directly on the centerline.

Distance measurements should be checked periodically by the person overseeing the fieldwork. Consistently over- or underestimating this variable will affect results. Borderline cases, in which the distance of the surveyed snag or tree falls on the edge of a width interval, need to be carefully checked. For example, if you estimate a tree to be 33 ft (10 m) away from the line, it is important to measure this distance exactly. Recording 33 ft (10 m) when the actual distance is 36 ft (11 m) biases the accuracy of your data. Estimating the distance by pacing often is accurate in open, flat areas, but for borderline cases, measuring the distance with a tape is required. In addition, when vegetation or steep terrain make pacing difficult, measure rather than estimate the distances to maintain accuracy.

Header row variables may also be recorded for each snag or tree encountered: (1) Forest, (2) District, (3) Subwatershed, (4) Observer, (5) Date, and (6) Pages. Because the data recorded for each of these variables may be redundant, the columns are set to the far right of the data entry spreadsheet. This enables easy viewing of the data while providing a permanent record of each of these variables for future referencing.

As with the log sampling protocol (Bate and others 2008), we recommend sampling 10 transects (4,000 ft or 1000 m) within each stratum for a pilot sample. For smaller trees and abundant snags, these samples are all that may be needed if the snag or tree size of interest is also normally distributed.

Although results from the pilot survey will identify an optimal plot length, we recommend continuing to sample afterwards with 400-ft or 100-m transects rather than switching to a shorter length, **unless** a serial correlation problem is detected (See "SnagPRO Analysis" section for more details). There are two reasons for this approach. First, snags and trees in different size classes usually differ in abundance and distribution; hence the optimal transect length for each differs. Second, most of the time required to sample snags and trees is to locate random points and establish transects. Transect lengths of 400 ft or 100 m are long enough to be efficient, yet short enough to ensure that sampling effort is not concentrated within a small area. Make sure to continue sampling with only the recommended width to save time in the field.

SnagPRO Analysis (Step 6)

In this section, we provide the general background, statistics, and discussion of each function and page within SnagPRO. Refer to the "Tutorial" section for detailed operating instructions and examples. See appendixes 3 and 4 for brief outlines of steps needed to conduct analyses on single-stratum and stratified landscapes, respectively.

No two data sets will be the same size. Data sets will differ depending on snag or tree characteristics, the abundance of qualifying snags or trees, number of strata, and the total number of samples taken. SnagPRO has been designed to accommodate these variations.

SnagPRO has been designed to accommodate variations in data sets including tree characteristics and abundance, number of strata, and number of samples.

Data entry—

To prepare for data entry and analysis, follow these steps:

1. Open the **Snag_Tutorial_Data.xls** file.
2. Activate the **Data Entry** sheet.
3. Click on **Move or Copy Sheet** under the **Edit** menu.
4. Check the box **Create a copy**.
5. Under **To book** click on (**new book**).
6. Rename the new file, and then use this sheet to make hardcopies for field-work.

To use hand-held computers during fieldwork, activate the data sheet and complete the process from step 3. Depending on the sampling objectives, not all fields on the data form may be necessary during field surveys or data entry, and you may choose to hide some columns. All mandatory columns, however, must be present (Unhide) in the CSV import file (fig. 5) or the SnagPRO import will fail.

To save the entered data as a CSV file:

1. Activate the **Data Entry** sheet.
2. Select **Save As** from the **File** menu.
3. Scroll to find CSV (comma delimited) (***.csv**).
4. Click **Save.**

Only the active sheet is saved. This keeps the original file intact, by saving the file with a different extension. Figure 5 illustrates the correct formatting needed to successfully import to SnagPRO.

Consecutive plots—
Scroll through the entire data set before importing it to SnagPRO to ensure that each transect has a unique numeric identifier and eight subsegment lengths, with the first subsegment numbered as "1." Otherwise, the analysis for optimal transect length will join subsegments from different transects.

Importing files—
To import data to SnagPRO, the application prompts users for some initial information. For example, the first message box to appear in SnagPRO asks users to indicate what habitat component will be analyzed:

- Logs
- Snags or Trees

Select **Snags or Trees** so that SnagPRO will expect the specific field names and column arrangement from the import file. SnagPRO opens the Snag and Tree Analysis portion. Selecting Logs will cause the SnagPRO import to fail. See Bate and others (2008) for correct formatting of log data.

This opens to a window that says "SnagPRO-Snag and Tree Analysis:"

1. From the **Measurement** menu, select **Metric** or **English**.
2. From the **File** menu, select **Open**.
3. Navigate to the location of the saved CSV data file, and select the file by clicking on **Open**.

Correctly formatted files will open promptly to the Single/Combined page in SnagPRO with the message, "Status: Data file read" in the bottom left-hand corner. This page is where the entire data set is stored while working in SnagPRO.

If SnagPRO fails to import the file, the message, "An invalid column header was found" will appear. If users know they selected the correct file to import the first time, there may be a problem with formatting. Copy the entire data set into a new file, including only the rows and columns with data. Then repeat the process above.

SnagPRO automatically inserts two "length" columns into the data set after a successful import, labeled Section and Segment. SnagPRO combines the subsegments of varying lengths into newly created sections and segments, resulting in four transect lengths: 50, 100, 200, and 400 ft, or 12.5, 25, 50, and 100 m. SnagPRO also inserts four "width" columns, labeled Width33, Width66, Width99, and Width132 for English, and Width10, Width20, Width30, and Width40 for metric measurement. These fields are later populated by your choice of formula. See "Formulas" below.

Default plot dimensions—

A user's sampling objectives may require different plot dimensions. To override SnagPRO's defaults, navigate to **Plot Dimensions** and select **Custom Dimensions**, then place the cursor within each box to enter the correct length(s) and/or width(s). Remember that for optimal transect length analyses, transects should be twice as long as sections, sections twice as long as segments, and segments twice as long as subsegments.

> **For optimal transect length analyses, transects should be twice as long as sections, sections twice as long as segments, and segments twice as long as subsegments.**

Preselected transect lengths and widths—

For analyses using a single transect length and width, navigate to **Settings** and select **Optimal Selection**. Check the plot dimension to be included in the analysis. Check **Automatic** to again include all plot sizes in the analysis. If you did not collect data using long transects, but wanted only segment lengths, data entry must follow the same protocol for SnagPRO analysis. That is, still identify each transect with a unique numeric identifier, and then divide into smaller subsegments. During the CSV import, SnagPRO creates and populates the Segment column, so users only need to check it to include it for the analysis.

Species—

Users may select from three options for analyzing snag or tree data by species:

1. All species
2. One species, excluding all others
3. Exclude a single species

SnagPRO's default values include all species in the analysis, providing a choice to exclude a single species (**Multiple** button). For analysis of a single species, select **Single** at the bottom of the screen.

Formulas

SnagPRO evaluates each snag or tree by using five criteria for data entries before a value based on a formula is placed in each of the width columns:

1. D.b.h.
2. Height
3. Class: decay (snags) or structural (trees)
4. Species
5. Distance

The first four criteria are relative fields. The values accepted are those entered by the user.

The distance criterion is an absolute field. SnagPRO truncates the distances for each snag or tree in 16.5-ft (5-m) intervals from the centerline, creating four plot widths. These four plot widths correspond to the four width columns that are blank.

SnagPRO's formulas are "If, then" statements. **If** the snag or tree meets all criteria specified by the user, **plus** meets the distance requirement, **then** a "1" is placed in that specific width column. **If** the snag or tree fails to meet all specified criteria, **then** it places a "0" in the column.

Only those snags or trees meeting **all** requirements of the user-created formula receive a "1" and are included in the statistical analysis for each plot size. For example, if the perpendicular distance (half width) of a snag from the centerline was measured at 23 ft (7 m) and it meets all other criteria, the snag qualifies for the Width66(20), Width99(30), and Width132(40) columns. The snag is not included in the Width33(10) column because it falls beyond that width interval around the centerline. The Width33(10) column represents a plot with a 33-ft (10-m) total width, or a 16.5-ft (5-m) half width. Only snags or trees ≤16.5 ft (5 m) away from the centerline, in either direction, will be accepted within the Width33(10) column. See figures 2 and 3 as examples.

SnagPRO evaluates d.b.h. and height characteristics based on the minimum value the user provides, and decay or structural classes based on a maximum value specified by the user. Decay values are based on Cline and others (1980), who considered decay classes I through III as hard snags, and decay classes IV and V as soft snags, based on their five-decay-class system. If only hard snags are to be included, enter a "3" as the maximum value.

Parks and others (1997) reduced the total number of decay classes to three by combining Cline and other's (1980) decay classes 2 and 3, and classes 4 and 5. The division between hard and soft snags therefore remains the same, so the two systems are compatible. Bull and others (1997) also provided descriptions of large-tree structural variations important to wildlife. For example, hollow trees, trees with partial decay, and trees with brooms provide valuable wildlife habitats. Use of structural classes can include such important information.

We recommend referring to Bull and others (1997) before starting a large-tree survey to ensure that large-tree structural classes are designed to meet objectives. See appendix 2 for an example. Values used for large-tree structural classes should be arranged so that with increasing values, the tree is increasingly sound. This is the opposite of the decay class values for snags.

Cavity and Foraging Signs

The objectives of snag or tree sampling may include collection of data on wildlife use. For example, to determine the snag species in which most of the cavities exist, use SnagPRO's **Cavity** function. Or, to determine which tree species exhibits the most foraging, choose **Forage** for your analysis.

To determine a value for Percent Use, each function evaluates every snag or tree for the following five factors:

1. D.b.h.
2. Height.
3. Class: decay (snag) or structural (tree).
4. Species.
5. Cavity or foraging use.

Percent Use is calculated by dividing the number of snags or trees with cavities or foraging signs by the total number of snags or trees encountered.

$$P_u = \frac{S_s}{S_t} \qquad (1)$$

where

P_u = percentage of use,

S_s = number of snags or trees with nesting or foraging signs, and

S_t = total number of snags or trees encountered.

In the field, it is not always possible to determine whether a snag or tree has a cavity because the bole is partially hidden. To exclude such snags in the calculation of percentage use, leave the cell blank.

Few subwatersheds will be homogeneous enough to forgo stratification.

Sorting Data Sets

Few subwatersheds will be homogeneous enough to forgo stratification. In addition, the optimal plot size will likely differ among heterogeneous strata, because of differences in the means and variances. Consequently, data need to be separated so that each stratum can be analyzed individually. SnagPRO automatically sorts data sets into separate strata once the Single or Multiple button is clicked and values are placed in the Width columns. The entire data set is retained on the Single/Combined page.

SnagPRO automatically sorts data into separate strata so that each stratum can be analyzed individually. The entire data set remains on the Single/Combined page and can be analyzed as a single stratum. This is helpful for situations in which it is not certain whether stratification was helpful in increasing precision.

Analysis for Nonstratified Stand or Landscape

Before means, standard deviations, and sample sizes are computed, the values in the Width columns need to be summed and subtotaled for each of the four transect lengths. The means, standard deviations, current number of samples, and sample size required are then calculated from these values.

Once the Width columns are populated, sum the qualifying snags or trees for a **nonstratified stand or landscape** with these steps:
1. Click on the **Optimal** tab.
2. Select **Single** in the "Stratum to Process" section (highlight the circle).
3. Click **Compute**.

SnagPRO calculates subtotals, displaying the average, standard deviation (std. dev.), and current number of samples (N) for each plot size on the Summary Statistics page. These calculated averages, standard deviations, and current number of samples also are copied to the Optimal page.

Analysis for individual strata on a stratified landscape—
Sum the qualifying snags or trees for each stratum on a stratified landscape with these steps:
1. Click on the **Optimal** tab.
2. Select **Stratum 1** in the "Stratum to Process" section.
3. Click **Compute**.

SnagPRO prompts users for:
- Number of strata
- Numeric code for the General Cost per Sample Guideline (see the "Optimal Plot Size" section for details) for stratum 1
- Size of each stratum (acres or hectares).

Repeat the process above for each additional stratum. Again, the results are displayed on the Summary Statistics and Optimal pages.

Averages are calculated by using the equation:

$$\overline{x} = \frac{\sum x_i}{n}$$ (2)

where

$\overline{x}$ = sample mean,

x_i = value of x observed in sample *i,* and

n = total number of samples.

Standard deviations are obtained by the equation:

$$s = \sqrt{\frac{n\sum x_i^2 - \left(\sum x_i\right)^2}{n(n-1)}}$$ (3)

where

s = sample standard deviation.

Optimal Plot Size

After running the summary statistics, SnagPRO provides the information on the Optimal page to aid users in selecting the optimal plot size. The statistics for each subsegment, segment, section, and transect within a unique stratum are displayed across three consecutive pages. For each stratum, the optimal plot size analysis needs to be run separately. The Stratum box immediately above the Optimal tabs allows for a text description of the stratum, which is useful when working with different size classes and for multiple strata. Users may print these results before proceeding to other strata.

There are two options to determine the optimal plot size for a stratum or area. The sample size option examines the number of plots required for sampling in comparison to the number of acres or hectares that would be sampled using that plot size. The second option is Wiegert's (1962) method, which incorporates a cost factor into the analysis. Default settings for both options estimate the number of samples needed to obtain a density estimate that is within 20 percent of the true mean, 90 percent of the time.

The sample size option considers three factors:

- The sample size required in plots.
- The sample size required in acres (ha).
- Whether the estimated sample size (n) meets the minimum requirements.

The required sample size (Cochran 1977) is determined by:

$$n = \left(\frac{t_\alpha s}{d}\right)^2$$ (4)

Weigert's method incorporates a cost factor into sample size analysis.

where

n = sample size required to estimate the mean density,

s = standard deviation of the mean within each plot size,

t_α = student's t-value for a 90-percent confidence interval ($\alpha = 0.10$), and

d = desired absolute error (calculated as 20 percent of the pilot mean).

After selecting **Optimal 2** tab, locate the required number of sample plots in the Sample Size (plots) column. Then this number is converted to the area requirements and reported in the Sample Size (acres [ha]) column.

The optimal plot size typically is one that requires sampling the minimal number of plots and acres (ha), once the requirements are met, but several sizes may be appropriate. Results from the pilot sample should enable users to determine if it is more efficient and accurate to use a wider or a narrower plot width, given the forest conditions of this stratum.

Example: Results on the Optimal 2 sheet estimate that a Section length with a 132-ft (40-m) plot width requires 20 acres (49 ha) more than one that is only 66 ft (20 m) wide to obtain the same level of precision. This difference may or may not take a considerable amount of time to survey, depending on sampling conditions. In areas where snags or trees are present in low densities, and visibility is open to 66 ft (20 m) from the centerline, the Section lengths that are 132 ft (40 m) wide would probably be the best choice to ensure that every possible snag is surveyed. By contrast, if snag or tree densities are moderate or high, narrower plots are likely the better choice. This will reduce sampling effort by decreasing the amount of time required to complete each plot.

Users also need to consider how difficult it is to see and reach snags or trees out to the specified distance. In steep terrain where shorter snags may be obscured by vegetation, it is important to select a narrower plot size to maintain accuracy.

The option that incorporates Wiegert's (1962) method demonstrates that the optimal plot size is that which minimizes the product of the Relative Cost and the Relative Variance. If both relative costs and variances are available, Wiegert's method is considered preferable (Krebs 1989).

Although it is more accurate to estimate costs by conducting time trials, there are some logistical difficulties. Time trials are conducted by surveying one plot size at a time, and cannot be conducted simultaneously with the pilot survey, which usually requires surveying snags or large trees to 66 ft (20 m) from the centerline. Consequently, the time and costs to conduct time trials may quickly offset any benefits because of the additional field effort required beyond the pilot survey. Therefore, we recommend against conducting time trials. Instead, we suggest using the cost factors provided in SnagPRO, which were developed on a relative scale. We have outlined our methods below so that users may understand how the costs were derived.

There are six cost scenarios in SnagPRO. Click on **Compute** and choose the category that best describes the forest situation within each stratum to see how the relative cost affects the outcome of your decision about the optimal plot size. The cost data are transferred to the Optimal page. Try several Costs per Sample categories if forest conditions are between categories.

We modified Wiegert's method by calculating the total cost expected for each plot size selected. This is valuable information, because all costs are relative to each other within the same area. Total cost also incorporates the minimum sample size required. Although the actual cost for sampling will vary for a particular area, selecting the plot size that demonstrates the lowest total cost allows users to select the optimal plot size for the forest conditions sampled.

Estimating Costs

The cost per plot is mainly a function of three factors: visibility, terrain, and density. Visibility is the unobstructed viewing distance from centerline to snags or trees for a given stratum. It is most strongly affected by seral stage or young tree or shrub cover within a stand. Terrain includes slope, young tree or shrub cover, and density of logs, all of which affect difficulty in traversing an area. Density is the number of snags or trees per unit area for a given size class of interest. Stands of higher density will require substantially more time, and thus higher costs, to sample.

Each survey has an associated fixed cost and a cost estimate for each plot, calculated at $10 per observer/hour. Fixed Cost is the time spent selecting and locating each beginning transect point, including the time spent returning to a vehicle upon completion. Costs may be minimal in clearcut areas or quite high in areas with difficult terrain. We therefore calculated an average fixed cost for each of the four possible plot lengths (transect, section, segment, and subsegment) based on a moderate situation with a low snag density.

SnagPRO's cost estimates were based on time trials conducted in forests in northern Idaho, adjusted with cost estimates from a snag study in the central Oregon Cascade Range. During the time trials, all snags >10 in (25 cm) d.b.h. were surveyed. For each snag, we recorded the following snag characteristics: species, d.b.h. (measured with a Biltmore diameter stick), decay class, height (ocular estimate), distance of the midpoint of the snag from the centerline, nesting evidence (ocular), and foraging signs (ocular).

In flat, open areas, distances to each snag were either paced or measured with a tape. Paced distances were calibrated with a measuring tape to ensure accurate and

---

The cost per plot is mainly a function of three factors: visibility, terrain, and density.

precise estimation of distances. Paced distances, following calibration, were then used to count snags that were clearly within the plot width, but snags potentially on the boundary, referred to as "marginal," were always measured with a tape. For example, a snag was considered marginal if its distance of 16.5 or 18 ft (5 or 5.5 m) away from the line was uncertain. For these cases, all distances were measured. In addition, periodic calibration of pacing was conducted. In steep areas, all distances >12 ft (3.5 m) were measured.

We developed six hypothetical situations based on three categories of terrain and snag visibility coupled with two snag densities. "Easy" refers to an area that is relatively flat (<30 percent slope) and where snags or trees are easily observed to 66 ft (20 m) in both directions. "Moderate" refers to situations where the slope is 30 to 50 percent and visibility of snags or trees averages 50 ft (15 m). "Difficult" describes situations in which a combination of factors makes travel difficult and slow and visibility is low. In dense regeneration stands, it is not possible to accurately detect snags beyond a particular distance. Travel could be difficult owing to slope, type of seral stage, amount of shrub cover, or density of logs.

Cost estimates were then developed for each forest situation given two densities:

* Low—two snags per acre (0.8 snags/ha).
* High—eight snags per acre (3.2 snags/ha) as shown in table 2.

Total time was computed by summing:

* Average time required for an observer to walk a 164-ft (50-m) line while looking for snags in the various forest conditions, without encountering any snags.
* Average amount of time per snag in the different forest conditions needed to record the seven snag characteristics listed above.

Total time was then multiplied by $10 per hour to obtain the cost estimate (table 2). Costs for all other transect lengths were derived either by doubling the cost, or dividing by 2, for the shorter lengths. These costs where then placed into the General Cost per Sample Guidelines tables found under the View menu in SnagPRO for both English (table 3) and metric (table 4) analyses. Note that costs jump substantially within the moderate and difficult categories for the Width99(30) and Width132(40) plot sizes, owing to the observer having to periodically leave the centerline to survey beyond the point of visibility.

One of the basic assumptions of all analyses presented here is that sampling units are independent

Analysis for independence—
One of the basic assumptions of all analyses presented here is that sampling units are independent (Hurlbert 1984, Krebs 1989, Swihart and Slade 1985). This means

Table 2—Cost estimates based on time trials to conduct snag (≥10-in [25-cm] diameter at breast height) surveys in different forest conditions

Visibility,[a] terrain,[b] density[c]	Plot dimensions	Time to walk plot length (no snags)	Average number of snags per plot	Time per snag	Total time	Total cost[d]
		Minutes		*- - - Minutes - - -*		*Dollars*
High,	Section33(10)	2	0 .25	2	2.50	0.43
easy,	Section66(20)	2	.50	2	3.00	.51
low	Section99(30)	2	.75	2	3.50	.60
	Section132(40)	2	1.00	2	4.00	.68
High,	Section33(10)	2	1.00	2	4.00	.68
easy,	Section66(20)	2	2.00	2	6.00	1.02
high	Section99(30)	2	3.00	2	8.00	1.36
	Section132(40)	2	4.00	2	10.00	1.70
Medium,	Section33(10)	3	.25	3	3.75	.64
moderate,	Section66(20)	3	.50	3	4.50	.77
low	Section99(30)	4.5	.75	3	6.75	1.15
	Section132(40)	6.75	1.00	3	9.75	1.66
Medium,	Section33(10)	3	1.00	3	5.00	.85
moderate,	Section66(20)	3	2.00	3	8.00	1.36
high	Section99(30)	4.5	3.00	3	13.50	2.30
	Section132(40)	6.75	4.00	3	18.75	3.19
Low,	Section33(10)	6	.25	4	7.0	1.19
difficult,	Section66(20)	6	.50	4	8.0	1.36
low	Section99(30)	24	.75	4	27.0	4.59
	Section132(40)	30	1.00	4	34.0	5.78
Low,	Section33(10)	6	1.00	4	10.0	1.70
difficult,	Section66(20)	6	2.00	4	14.0	2.38
high	Section99(30)	24	3.00	4	36.0	6.12
	Section132(40)	30	4.00	4	46.0	7.82

Note: Section33(10) = 33 ft (10 m) wide, section66(20) = 66 ft (20 m) wide, section 99(30) = 99 ft (30 m) wide, section132(40) = 132 ft (40 m) wide.

[a] High is ≥66 ft (20 m); medium is 49.5 ft (15 m); low is <33 ft (10 m).

[b] Easy is ≤30 percent slope, moderate is >30 but <50 percent slope; difficult is ≥50 percent slope.

[c] Low = 2 snags/ac (0.8/ha), high = 8 snags/ac (3.2/ha).

[d] Cost calculated at $10 per hour per person.

Table 3—Cost per sample using English-unit plots

Plot dimensions[a]	1 Easy,[b] low density[c]	2 Easy, high density	3 Moderate, low density	4 Moderate, high density	5 Difficult, low density	6 Difficult high density
	Dollars per sample					
Subsegment33	0.13	0.21	0.20	0.26	0.36	0.52
Subsegment66	0.16	0.31	0.23	0.41	0.41	0.73
Subsegment99	0.18	0.41	0.35	0.70	1.40	1.87
Subsegment132	0.21	0.52	0.51	0.97	1.76	2.38
Segment33	0.26	0.41	0.39	0.52	0.73	1.04
Segment66	0.31	0.62	0.47	0.83	0.83	1.45
Segment99	0.37	0.83	0.70	1.40	2.80	3.73
Segment132	0.41	1.04	1.01	1.95	3.52	4.77
Section33	0.52	0.83	0.78	1.04	1.45	2.07
Section66	0.62	1.24	0.94	1.66	1.66	2.90
Section99	0.73	1.66	1.40	2.80	5.60	7.46
Section132	0.83	2.07	2.02	3.89	7.05	9.54
Transect33	1.05	1.66	1.56	2.07	2.90	4.15
Transect66	1.24	2.49	1.88	3.32	3.32	5.80
Transect99	1.46	3.32	2.80	5.61	11.20	14.93
Transect132	1.66	4.15	4.05	7.78	14.10	19.07

[a] Dimensions are 33, 66, 99, or 132 ft wide.
[b] Easy is ≤30 percent slope; moderate is >30 but <50 percent slope; difficult is ≥50 percent slope.
[c] Low density = 2 snags/ac, high density = 8 snags/ac.

Table 4—Costs per sample using metric-unit plots

Plot dimensions[a]	1 Easy,[b] low density[c]	2 Easy, high density	3 Moderate, low density	4 Moderate, high density	5 Difficult, low density	6 Difficult high density
	Dollars per sample					
Subsegment10	0.11	0.17	0.16	0.21	0.30	0.43
Subsegment20	0.13	0.26	0.19	0.34	0.34	0.60
Subsegment30	0.15	0.34	0.29	0.58	1.15	1.53
Subsegment40	0.17	0.43	0.42	0.80	1.45	1.96
Segment10	0.22	0.34	0.32	0.43	0.60	0.85
Segment20	0.26	0.51	0.39	0.68	0.68	1.19
Segment30	0.30	0.68	0.58	1.15	2.30	3.06
Segment40	0.34	0.85	0.83	1.60	2.89	3.91
Section10	0.43	0.68	0.64	0.85	1.19	1.70
Section20	0.51	1.02	0.77	1.36	1.36	2.38
Section30	0.60	1.36	1.15	2.30	4.59	6.12
Section40	0.68	1.70	1.66	3.19	5.78	7.82
Transect10	0.86	1.36	1.28	1.70	2.38	3.40
Transect20	1.02	2.04	1.54	2.72	2.72	4.76
Transect30	1.20	2.72	2.30	4.60	9.18	12.24
Transect40	1.36	3.40	3.32	6.38	11.56	15.64

[a] Dimensions are 10, 20, 30, or 40 m wide.
[b] Easy is ≤30 percent slope; moderate is >30 and <50 percent slope; difficult is ≥50 percent slope.
[c] Low density is <0.8 snags/ha, high density is >3.2 snags/ha.

that whatever length of transect is chosen as optimal (subsegments, segments, or sections), the user can assume that the snag density in one sampling unit is not predicted by the snag density on the previous sampling unit of the same transect. Sampling units that are serially correlated would violate the assumption of sampling independence (Krebs 1989).

SnagPRO tests for serial correlations between increments of similar length along transects. Users will find this function on the Summary Statistics page. To conduct the test:

1. Fill in the Width columns on the **Single/Combined** page by using the appropriate formula (**Single** or **Multiple**).
2. **Compute** statistics on the **Optimal** page for the stratum of interest.
3. Click **Correlation** on the Summary Statistics page.
4. Enter the name of the transect length increment to test for serial correlation.
5. Enter the width of the plot size you are interested in testing.

Results provide a Pearson's correlation coefficient and the coefficient of determination. The correlation coefficient (r) estimates the strength of linear association between two variables (Sokal and Rohlf 1981). The coefficient of determination (r^2) is the correlation coefficient squared. It estimates the linear dependence of one variable upon another. In this instance, the r^2 value indicates how much the density in one transect increment is predicted by another transect increment.

The range for correlation coefficients is -1 to +1 (Sokal and Rohlf 1981). A high correlation coefficient suggests that adjacent increments along the same transect (for example, subsegments, segments, or sections) are correlated with each other and cannot be considered independent sampling units.

As a general guide, a correlation coefficient <0.45 ($r^2 < 0.2$) suggests that adjacent increments are independent and the increment selected can be used as the sampling unit. Values higher than this suggest adjacent increments are correlated. In the latter case, alternative transect lengths (combined segments or subsegments) must be tested for independence, and this process continued until an optimal transect length is identified that is not serially correlated.

> **Generally, a correlation coefficient <0.45 suggests that adjacent increments are independent and the increment selected can be used as the sampling unit.**

Sample Size Determination

The estimated sample size for unstratified subwatersheds is found under Sample Size (plots) of Optimal 2 tab. For stratified subwatersheds, go to the Sample Size page. SnagPRO provides both the proportional allocation and optimal methods for estimating the total sample size required, identified as the number of plots and acres (ha) required for sampling within each stratum.

The proportional allocation method allocates the samples among the strata based on the proportion of the total area in each stratum (weight W_i). By contrast, optimal allocation incorporates both the stratum proportional area (W_i) and variance (s_i^2) to determine the number of samples required within each stratum (Krebs 1989). Both methods calculate the number of samples required to obtain a density estimate within 20 percent of the true mean 90 percent of the time.

The sample size (Krebs 1989) required by the proportional allocation method is determined by the equation:

$$n = \frac{t_\alpha^2 \sum W_i s_i^2}{B^2} \tag{5}$$

where

B = desired bound for 1 - α ($x_{st} \cdot$ 20 percent),[1]

t_α = student's t value for 90-percent confidence limits (1 - α),

n = total sample size required in stratified sampling,

W_i = stratum weight (A_i/A), and

s_i^2 = variance in stratum I.

Then the number of samples within each stratum (n_i) is determined by multiplying the total number of samples needed (n) by the weight (W_i) of each stratum.

$$n_i = nW_i \tag{6}$$

Sample size for the optimal allocation method (Krebs 1989) is found by using the following equation:

$$n = \frac{\left(\sum W_i s_i\right)^2}{\left(\dfrac{B}{t_\alpha}\right)^2 + \left(\dfrac{1}{A}\right)\left(\sum W_i s_i^2\right)} \tag{7}$$

where

A = total number of acres (ha) in subwatershed, and

s_i = standard deviation in stratum i.

Then the number of samples needed within each stratum is estimated by:

$$n_i = n\left(\frac{A_i s_i}{\sum A_i s_i}\right) \tag{8}$$

---

[1] We have substituted the symbol B (to denote bound) for the d listed in Krebs (1989) equations.

where

A_i = number of acres (ha) in stratum i, and

n_i = total sample size required in stratum i.

Both allocation methods have advantages and disadvantages. Proportional allocation offers the advantage of dropping the strata and combining all samples after sampling is done, which is appropriate when there is little or no difference in densities among strata. This yields a larger sample size (n) and a smaller variance (s^2). This option is not available if the optimal allocation method is used. Optimal allocation, however, provides the best estimate for the least cost in situations where large differences in density exist among strata. With this method, sampling is concentrated in the stratum that has highest variance. By contrast, proportional allocation concentrates sampling effort in the largest stratum, regardless of the variance within each stratum.

Again, remember that the sample sizes given are only estimates of the number required to obtain a desired level of precision. Consequently, data should be analyzed in SnagPRO periodically to gauge the precision of estimates.

Estimating Densities

A minimum of 60 samples for the landscape, or 20 samples from each stratum (whichever is higher), are required before the mean density of snags or trees can be estimated. At this point, users can decide whether enough samples have been collected to achieve their objectives. See the earlier section, "Establishing Transects," which describes an exception to the above requirements for sample size.

The two density options provided are **Estimate Average Density** and **Compare to Target Density**. The first allows users to obtain an average snag or tree density that is within 20 percent of the true mean at a desired confidence level. The second allows users to determine whether the estimated density is significantly different from the targeted density. Users may choose both options. Go to the Densities page to use the Estimate Average Density option. For the Compare to Target Density option, you must first obtain a density estimate from the Densities page, and transfer this information to the Statistical Test page.

Estimate Average Density

The Estimate Average Density option requires one of two equations based on which sampling method you use: simple or stratified random sampling. To see these equations, go to the Densities page.

For the simple random sampling method, the average is calculated in the standard way (equation 2). Then the variance is calculated by:

Estimate Average Density allows users to obtain an average snag or tree density that is within 20 percent of the true mean at a desired confidence level. Compare to Target Density allows users to determine whether the estimated density is significantly different from the targeted density.

$$s^2 = \frac{\sum (x_i - \overline{x})^2}{n - 1} \tag{9}$$

and the standard error of the mean is determined by:

$$s_{\overline{x}} = \sqrt{\frac{s^2}{n}} \tag{10}$$

where

$\overline{x}$ = population mean,

x_i = observed x value in sample i,

n = sample size,

s^2 = variance of the measurements, and

$s_{\overline{x}}$ = standard error of the mean $\overline{x}$.

The confidence interval is then calculated using a normal approximation (Krebs 1989):

$$\overline{x} \pm t_\alpha \, s_{\overline{x}} \tag{11}$$

where

t_α = student's t value for 90-percent confidence limits (1 - α).

The t-value is preset at 1.67 for a sample size equal to 60 ($n = 60$) to obtain a 90-percent confidence interval. If a different level of confidence is desired, the t-value may be changed. On the Simple-Random Sampling Equation page, an estimated mean is given based on simple random sampling methods.

In the second method, a density estimate with a bound is calculated based on stratified random sampling methods. The stratified mean density is computed by the following equation:

$$\overline{x}_{st} = \frac{\sum_{i=1}^{L} A_i \overline{x}_i}{A} \tag{12}$$

where

$\overline{x}_{st}$ = stratified population mean (number per acres [ha]),

$\overline{x}_i$ = observed mean in stratum i,

A_i = number of acres (ha) in stratum i,

A = total number of acres (ha) in subwatershed,

i = stratum number, and

L = total number of strata.

To calculate a confidence interval, the stratified variance must first be determined:

$$\text{Variance of } (\overline{x}_{st}) = \sum_{i=1}^{L} \left(\frac{W_i^2 \ s_i^2}{n_i} \right) \qquad (13)$$

where

n_i = number of samples in stratum i,

s_i^2 = variance in stratum i, and

W_i = stratum weight or proportion of area in stratum i (A_i/A).

Then the confidence interval is calculated by the normal approximation:

$$\overline{x}_{st} \pm t_\alpha \left(\sqrt{\text{var } (\overline{x}_{st})} \right) \qquad (14)$$

Because SnagPRO is designed to accommodate landscapes with different numbers of strata, the user must enter the correct number when prompted by the "Number of Strata" message box. This tells SnagPRO which equation to use.

Compare to Target Density

The second density option is an informal statistical test that allows users to determine whether the estimated snag or tree density is significantly different from the targeted density, such as a targeted density identified in standards and guidelines for land use plans.

A minimum of 60 samples for the landscape, or 20 samples from each stratum (whichever is higher), are required. For subwatersheds >7,000 acres (2834 ha), it may be necessary to increase sampling effort to compensate for the natural variability of snags and trees in relation to elevation gradient.

An example is a 20,000-acre (8097-ha) subwatershed that encompasses three distinct forest community types; this situation may require about 100 samples to adequately conduct the compare-to-target-density test. This represents an increase of about three sample plots for every 1,000 acres (405 ha) surveyed above 7,000 acres (2834 ha). This option is especially useful in situations where densities are low and the sampling effort is extremely high to obtain an estimate within 20 percent of the true mean (90 percent of the time). It is intended for surveys where the main objective is to determine whether the subwatershed meets the targeted guidelines for retention of snags or large trees.

The t-test is the most common way to test for a significant difference between two means. The t-test compares the mean within each plot to the target mean. This works well in single-stratum landscapes, but there are some problems using this approach on stratified landscapes, where differences among multiple means must be tested. Consequently, SnagPRO calculates confidence intervals about each estimated mean snag density.

If the target mean falls within the confidence interval of the estimated mean, then the two values are not different, indicating management compliance with the target density.

If the target mean falls within the confidence interval of the estimated mean, then the two values are not different, indicating management compliance with the target density. If the target mean is significantly lower than the estimated mean density, this situation would also indicate management compliance. That is, the observed mean density is higher than the target density for management.

The Statistical Test page enables users to visually assess whether the estimated and targeted densities of a survey are significantly different from each other. Users simply enter the targeted density and the estimated density and its bounds from the snag or tree survey; results are automatically plotted on a graph. An example is a homogeneous 6,044-acre (2447-ha) area of ponderosa pine forest in the Oregon Cascade Range. The objective was to determine whether the area supported the targeted hard snag densities identified in the forest plan. The forest plan stipulated that the area support at least 0.9 hard snags per acre (2.2 hard snags/ha). On this site, the estimated (n = 175) hard snag density was 0.11 ± 0.04 snags per acre (0.3 ± 0.1 snags/ha [Bate 1995]). It was obvious that the area did not meet the targeted snag densities identified in the forest plan, as demonstrated statistically.

The null hypothesis for this test was:

H_0: There is no difference between the targeted and estimated hard snag densities.

To evaluate the results, we checked whether the target value (0.9 hard snags per acre [2.2 snags/ha]) fell between the values 0.07 and 0.15 on the Statistical Test page in SnagPRO (fig. 6). These values are the upper and lower limits on the mean estimate of 0.11 hard snags per acre (0.27 hard snags/ha). In this case, the targeted density did not fall within the confidence interval. We therefore rejected the null hypothesis. Because the target value was above the upper limit of the confidence (higher than the estimated mean density), we also concluded that snag density in the area did not comply with management direction.

These are the results when a 90-percent confidence interval is used. That is, there is a 90-percent probability that the estimated mean lies within the stated interval. If users want to increase the probability that a given interval will contain the true value of the estimated mean density, a 95- or a 99-percent confidence interval can be used (resulting in a 95-percent or 99-percent probability that the true value of the estimated mean lies within the interval). We recommend consulting with a statistician for more details regarding the choice of interval. In general, a 95-percent confidence interval is typically used for most analyses and considered appropriate for most situations where the cost is not prohibitive.

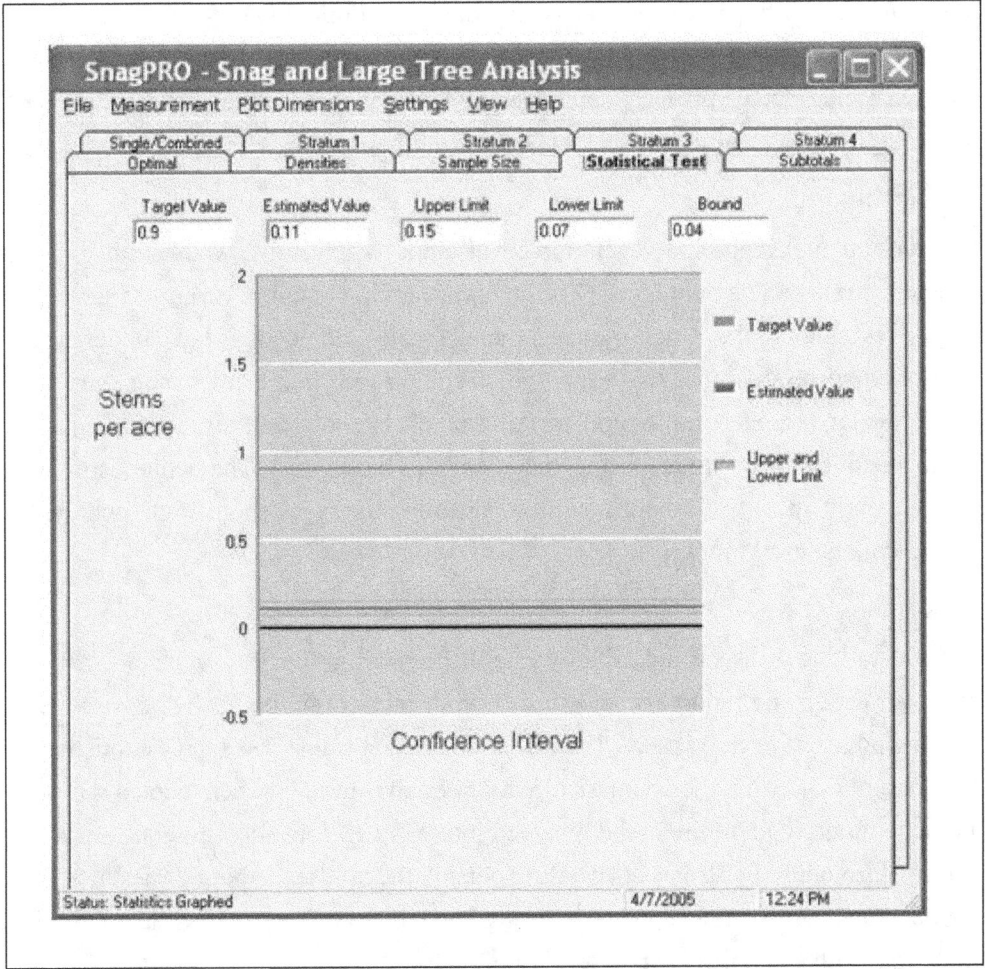

Figure 6—Statistical Test page. Results of the statistical test found a difference between the targeted density of 0.9 snags per acre (2.2 snags/ha) and the estimated density of 0.11 snags per acre (0.3 snags/ha). Data are from an area of intensive timber harvest in ponderosa pine forest on the Deschutes National Forest.

Tutorials

Example 1: Snag Density Analysis for Single-Stratum Landscape Using Metric Units

Background information—

A 364-ha stand of old-growth ponderosa pine, located on the east side of the central Oregon Cascade Range, is to be sampled to determine whether the area meets the targeted densities of hard snags dictated by the forest plan. The forest plan defines hard snags as those in decay classes I through III [Cline and others 1980]) that also are ≥25.4 cm d.b.h. and ≥1.8 m tall.

The forest plan dictates that at least 10 hard snags/ha be maintained to provide adequate nesting habitat. Also of interest is the estimated density of all snags in this same size class, to be used as baseline data for mimicking old-growth characteristics in adjacent areas. Therefore, sampling all decay classes is planned, but with hard snags as the primary objective. An additional objective is to estimate the percentage of snags (all decay classes) exhibiting new cavities.

Stratification—

Use aerial photographs and vegetation cover maps to determine whether any apparent strata can be delineated. The area appears to contain a variety of seral stages, owing to a mix of past management activities. Some areas have undergone controlled burns and others have not, which could result in different snag densities across the landscape. A more thorough ground check, however, reveals a relatively homogeneous forest with respect to snag densities based on 0.4-ha ocular estimates. Consequently, the area was not stratified. Visibility averages about 15 m, and the area is flat and easy to traverse.

Pilot survey—

Ten 100-m-long transects are initially established within the area by placing a grid over a map and randomly selecting 10 grid intersection points, which are the starting points of each transect. The direction of each transect is then established by randomly choosing the compass direction. Each transect is then labeled with a unique numeric identifier and delineated into eight 12.5-m subsegments, numbered 1 through 8. For transects heading outside the landscape boundaries, use the bounce-back method to keep the transect within the sampling area while continuing to sample with standardized transect lengths (fig. 4).

The Dataform sheet found in the file named Snag_Tutorial_Data.xls (fig. 5) is used as a hardcopy field form to record field data. See "Field Forms" under "General Surveying Procedures" for complete details. Appendix 2 can be customized to further explain to field crews what information and methods are required under each field heading.

In the field, all snags 20 m either side of the centerline of specified size are tallied within each subsegment. Distance is measured from the centerline to each snag's midpoint (that is, the center of a snag as opposed to the snag's outer bark area that is closest to centerline). For each snag, record:

- D.b.h. (cm)
- Height (m)
- Distance of the snag's midpoint from centerline (in meters)
- Numeric code for species
- Decay class (Cline and others 1980)
- Numeric codes are assigned to snags that have evidence of nesting. For

snags where it is not possible to determine whether a cavity exists because of vegetation, the cell is left blank (see app. 2 for details).

Data entry—
For this tutorial, the data are found in the Snag_Tutorial_Data.xls file on the Tutorial_data_I_metric page. This file can be found at the PNW Web site at http://www.fs.fed.us/pnw/publications/tools-databases.shtml. Open this file in the spreadsheet program Excel[2] for Windows. Ten transects of eight subsegments of data are available, following the same format provided on the field form (fig. 5).

Consecutive subsegments—
Before starting any analyses, sort transects and subsegments in ascending order to ensure that there are eight subsegments for each transect. In Excel, click **Data | Sort**, then select **Sort By Transect** and **Then By Subsegment**. Scroll through the entire data set to ensure that eight subsegment lengths have been entered for each transect, and the beginning subsegment of each transect is numbered "1."

Saving as a CSV file—
SnagPRO imports only CSV files. To create a CSV file, follow these steps:
1. Activate the **Tutorial_data_I_metric** sheet by clicking anywhere on the sheet: Select **File | Save As**.
2. Click **Save as Type** at the bottom of the Save As message box.
3. Select CSV (comma delimited) (***.csv**).
4. Assign a new file name in the file name box.
5. Click **Save**. When saved as a CSV file, only the active sheet is retained. Saving the file with a different name keeps the original file intact.

Importing to SnagPRO—
Import the CSV file of snag data by using these steps:
1. Launch SnagPRO by double-clicking on the desktop icon or the executable file—**SnagPRO .exe**.
2. Click **Snags or Trees**.
3. Go to **Measurement**, and click **Metric**.
4. Go to **File | Open**. In the message box "Look in," browse to the folder containing the CSV data and select the file name.

This should successfully import the CSV file. Note that additional columns have been added to your file:

---

[2] The use of trade or firm names in this publication is for reader information and does not imply endorsement by the U.S. Department of Agriculture of any product or service.

- The Segment and Section columns were inserted between Transect and Subsegment.
- Width10, Width20, Width30, and Width40 columns have been added.

SnagPRO combined consecutive subsegments (12.5-m lengths) into segments (25-m lengths), and segments into sections (50-m lengths). The Width columns are populated after you select a formula (see below).

Formula entry—

Create the appropriate formulas for the **Width** columns. These formulas determine which snags are included in the current analysis.

First obtain estimates of hard snags only. To do this, locate and click on the **Multiple** button on the Single/Combined page to have SnagPRO include multiple species in the analysis. Several input boxes will then appear.

To create the correct formula, based on your survey objectives, enter:

- "25.4" (cm) for D.b.h.
- "1.8" (m) for Height.
- "3" for Decay Class (hard snags based on Cline and others 1980).
- "9999" for Species (all species are included).

SnagPRO evaluates each snag for the criteria listed above plus its distance from the centerline. For snags meeting all criteria, a value of "1" is placed in the cell; otherwise, the cell receives a "0."

Analyzing by plot size—

SnagPRO now calculates means and standard deviations for each plot size, transferring the results to the Optimal pages. First, review General Cost per Sample Guidelines under the View menu to select one of the six cost categories that best applies to the forest conditions (see the "Estimating Costs" section for details). For this example, choose **Code 4** because the forest conditions have moderate visibility and terrain, and snag densities appear higher than 3.2 snags per hectare (table 4).

To sum and subtotal the values for each plot size, click the **Optimal** tab; go to **Stratum to Process**; select **Single,** and click **Compute.**

A series of message boxes will appear. Enter:

- "1" for the Number of Strata.
- "4" for the General Cost per Sample code.
- "364" (ha) for the Stratum Size.

SnagPRO calculates subtotals on the Summary Statistics page and simultaneously transfers the results to the Optimal page. On the bottom of the Summary Statistics page, you will find the mean, standard deviation, and current sample size for each plot size and length.

Optimal plot size—

To determine the plot size that optimizes sampling in the current forest conditions, switch to the Optimal page. There are three Optimal sheets. Activate the **Optimal 1** worksheet by clicking on this tab. Write a brief description of the study area in the shaded box labeled Stratum. For example, for this analysis you might write: "Old-growth; ≥25.4 cm d.b.h.; ≥1.8 m tall; hard snags."

On Optimal 1 tab, the Plot Dimensions column lists the 16 available plot sizes (fig. 7). The next column, Plot Size (meters ^2), displays the plot in square meters. Mean Density (#/plot) displays the estimated average for the 16 plot sizes, with the appropriate standard deviation values in Standard Deviation (#/plot).

Under Mean Density (#/hectare), the number of snags per plot is converted to the number of snags per hectare (fig. 7). Similarly, the standard deviation of each

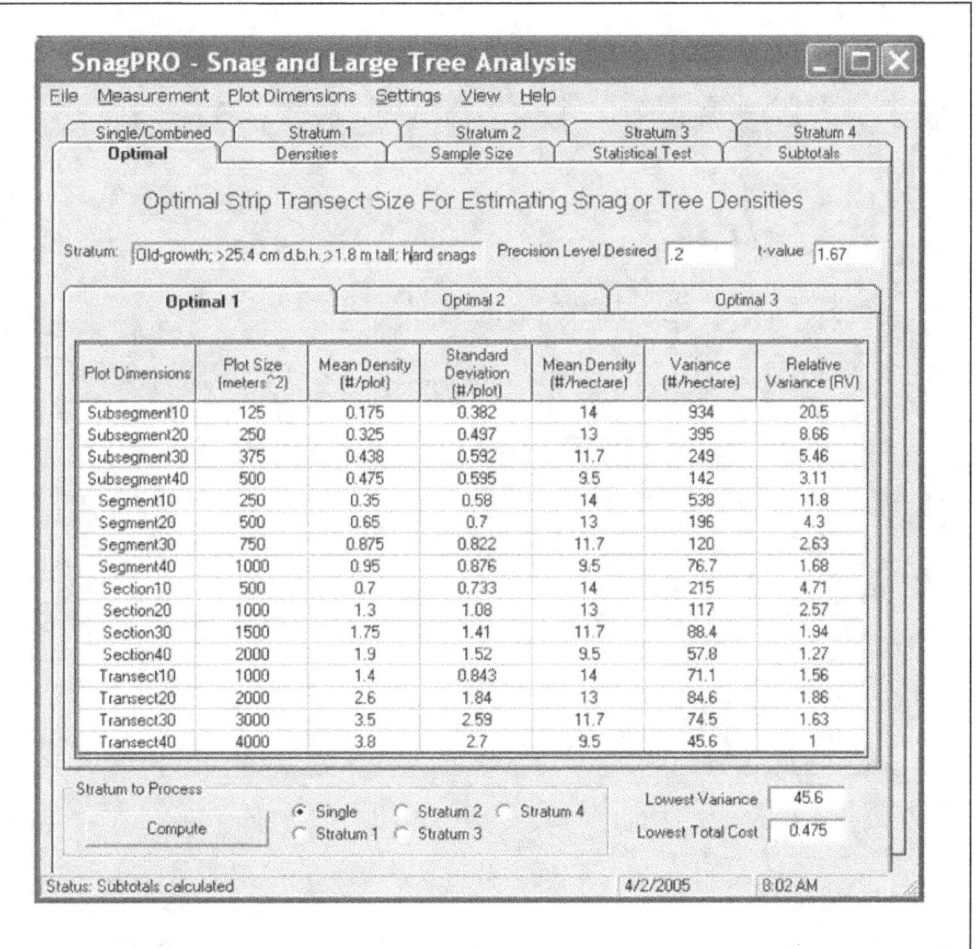

Figure 7—Optimal 1 page: first of three optimal pages showing size (m²), mean, standard deviation, variance, and relative variance for each plot size for hard snags in a single-stratum ponderosa pine landscape.

plot is squared to get the variance, and then converted to number per hectare in the Variance column. The mean snag density ranges from a low of 9.5 in the widest plots to a high of 14 in the narrowest plots. If you find that the density varies from low to high among plot widths, it is best to select one of the midrange plot widths so that you are not over- or underestimating snag densities. The Relative Variance column uses the lowest variance calculated among the 16 plot sizes as the divisor for all variances to determine the optimal plot size.

The **Optimal 2** tab page (fig. 8) repeats the first two columns from Optimal 1—Plot Dimensions and Plot Size (meters^2). Sample Size (plots) calculates the total number of plots and Sample Size (hectares) calculates the number of hectares needed to obtain a density estimate within 20 percent of the true mean 90 percent of the time, based on the sample mean and standard deviation.

Earlier, we stated that SnagPRO's equations require a minimum of 60 samples. The Minimum Number of Samples Required column represents the minimum

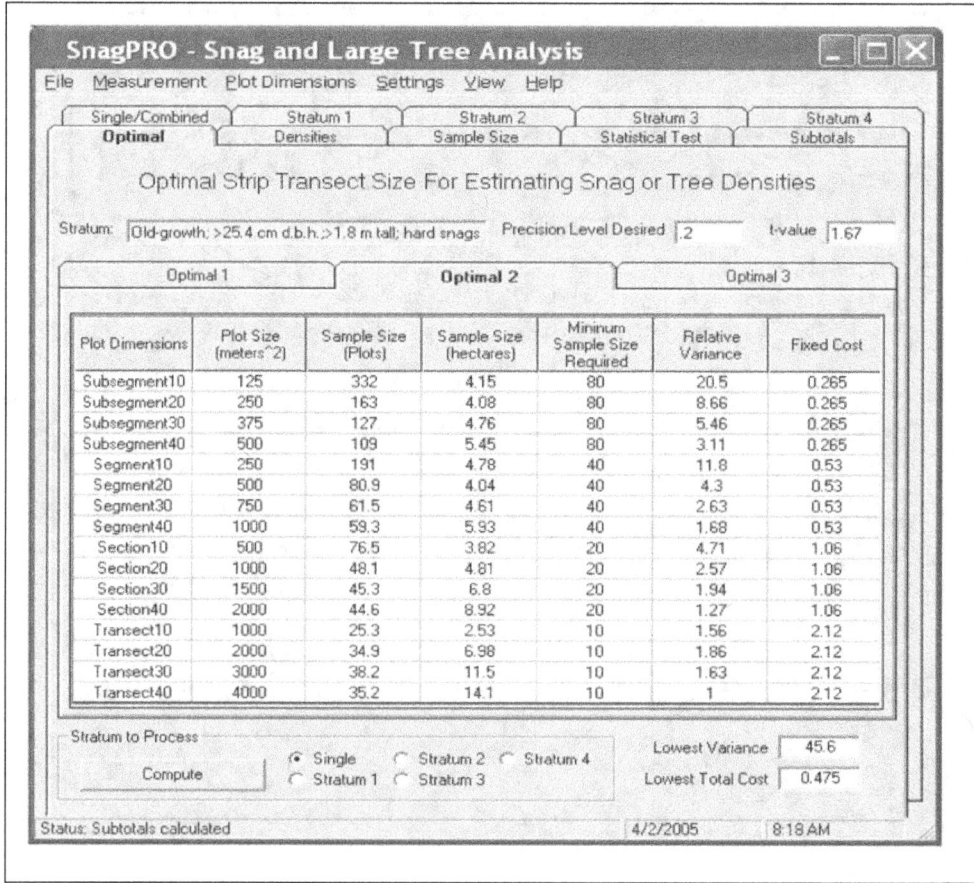

Figure 8—Optimal 2 page: second of three optimal pages showing sample size (plots), sample size (ha), minimum sample required, relative variance, and fixed cost for each plot size for hard snags in a single-stratum ponderosa pine landscape.

number of plots required for each transect length. See the "Establishing Transects" section for more detail on this subject. The final column in Optimal 2 gives the fixed cost associated with each plot size. See the "Estimating Costs" section for more detail.

The first two columns in **Optimal 3** (fig. 9) repeat each plot name and area. The Cost per Sample column reports the cost of each sample in addition to the Fixed Cost from Optimal 2, providing the Total Cost per Plot Unit.

SnagPRO calculates Relative Cost in the same way as Relative Variance from Optimal 1 and 2, dividing each total cost by the lowest cost in this column. Following Wiegert's method (1962), SnagPRO multiplies the relative variance by the relative cost to get Product. The optimal plot size is the one that minimizes the product of these two factors. Finally, the Total Cost column provides users with an idea of the costs they could expect for one plot size versus another.

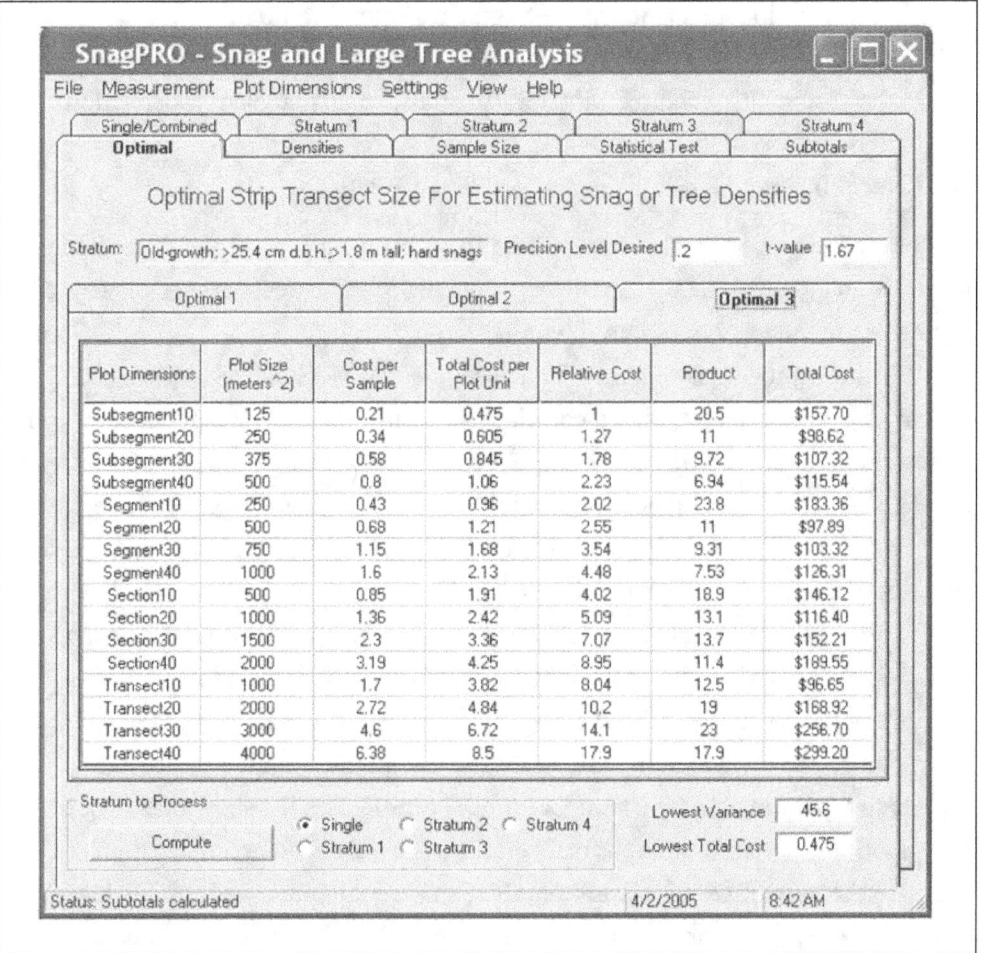

Figure 9—Optimal 3 page: third of three optimal pages showing cost per sample, total cost per plot unit, relative cost, product (cost x relative cost), and total cost for each plot size for hard snags in a single-stratum ponderosa pine landscape.

These variables are used in the decisionmaking process regarding sample design. On Optimal 2, review the number of plots required in **Sample Size (Plots)** for each **Plot Size (meters ^2)** (fig. 8). Which plot sizes require the fewest samples?

Consider the plot size in terms of area, as shown in Sample Size (hectares). Note that Transect10 requires the minimal number of plots (25.3) and hectares (2.53). Now check the Minimum Sample Size Required. With a sample size of only 10 it is not possible to assume a normal distribution because SnagPRO's equations work from a minimum of 60 samples.

Switch to **Optimal 3 | Total Cost** (fig. 9) to check the costs based on the minimum number of required samples. Transect10 plots could cost approximately $97; using Segment20 or Subsegment20 plots, the estimated total cost is similar, and these plots provide a larger sample size and thus would be a better choice, assuming these shorter transects are independent. To test for independence, switch to the **Summary Statistics** page and run the serial correlation test.

First test the independence of the Segment20 plots. To do this:

1. Click on the **Correlation** button in the bottom-right corner of the screen.
2. Enter "Segment" when the first message box appears labeled "Correlation Length."
3. Enter "20" into the box labeled "Correlation Width."

The message box displays the correlation coefficient ($r = 0.23$) and coefficient of determination ($r^2 = 0.05$). The low r^2 value (0.05) indicates that the adjacent 20-m segments are independent sampling units.

When this process is repeated for Subsegment20 plots, adjacent plots also appear to be independent, with a correlation coefficient (r) of 0.06 and a coefficient of determination (r^2) of 0.0. Thus, it is acceptable to use either plot size for analysis, but Subsegment20 plots appear to be slightly better. Because snags of all decay classes also are of interest, running the optimal plot analysis on both hard and soft snags may aid the decisionmaking process.

To analyze snags in all decay classes, return to **Single/Combined** page and click on the **Multiple** button. Refer to the "Formula Entry" section above and enter the same responses, with the exception of the decay class. Enter the value "5" instead of "3" to include both hard and soft snags in the analysis.

Go to **Optimal 1** and click on **Compute | Single**. Results show that snag densities for all decay classes are relatively high, ranging from an estimated 15 to 24 snags per hectare (fig. 10). In addition, the Sample Size (plots) required is low for a number of the plots as shown on Optimal 2 (fig. 11). This suggests a random distribution of snags (low variance) rather than a highly clumped one. For Subsegment20

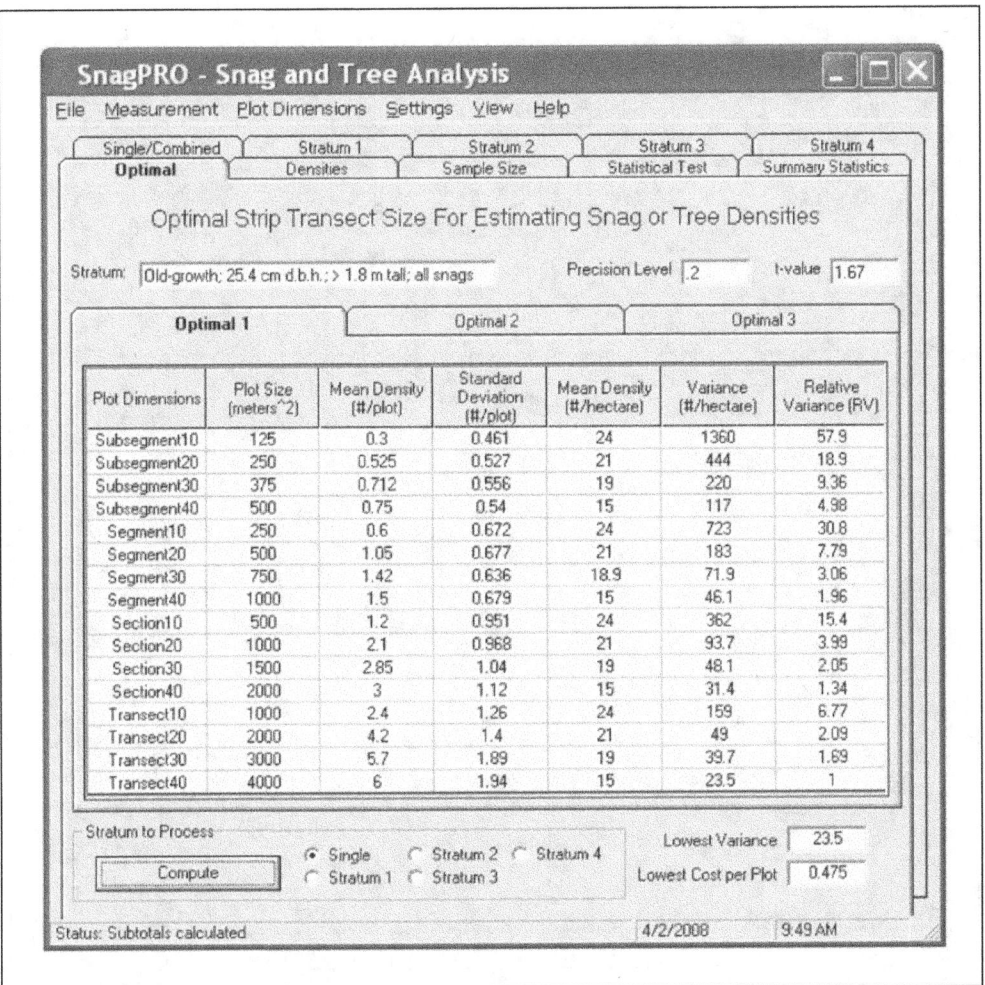

Figure 10—Optimal 1 page: first of three optimal pages showing size (m²), mean, standard deviation, variance, and relative variance for each plot size for both hard and soft snags in a single-stratum ponderosa pine landscape.

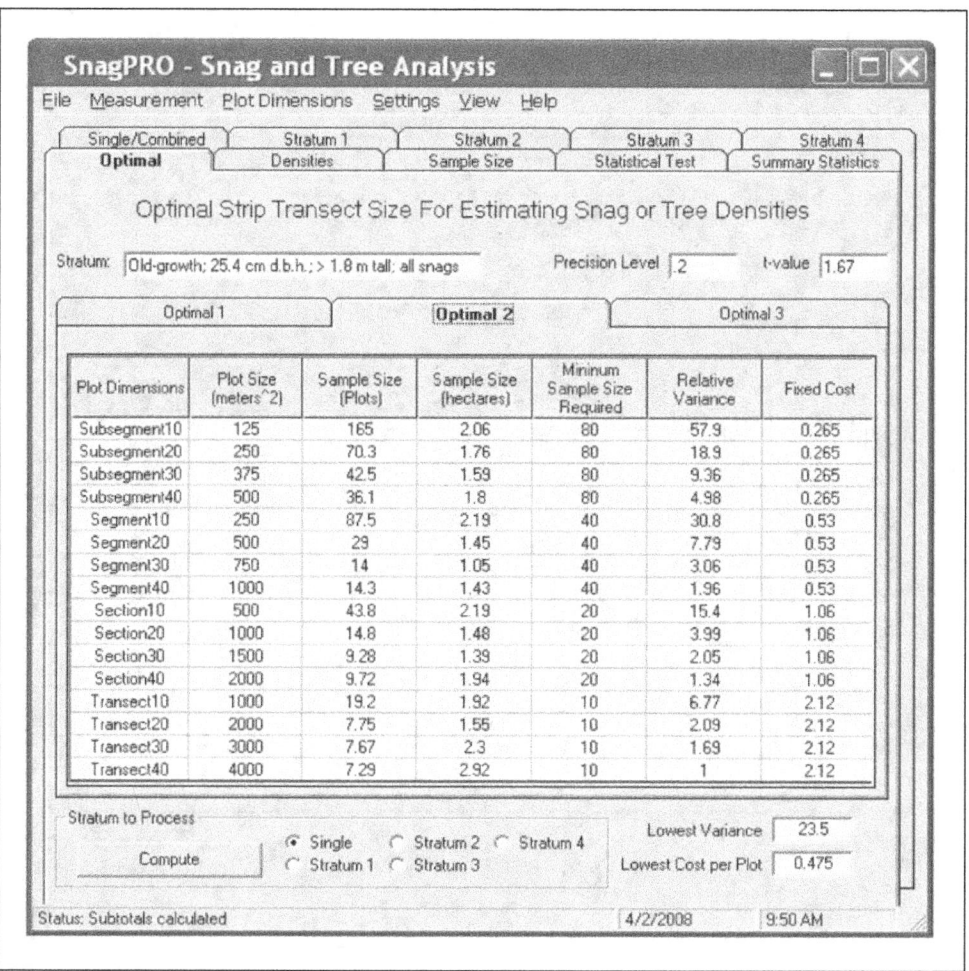

Figure 11—Optimal 2 page: second of three optimal pages showing sample size (plots), sample size (ha), minimum sample required, relative variance, and fixed costs for each plot size for both hard and soft snags in a single-stratum ponderosa pine landscape.

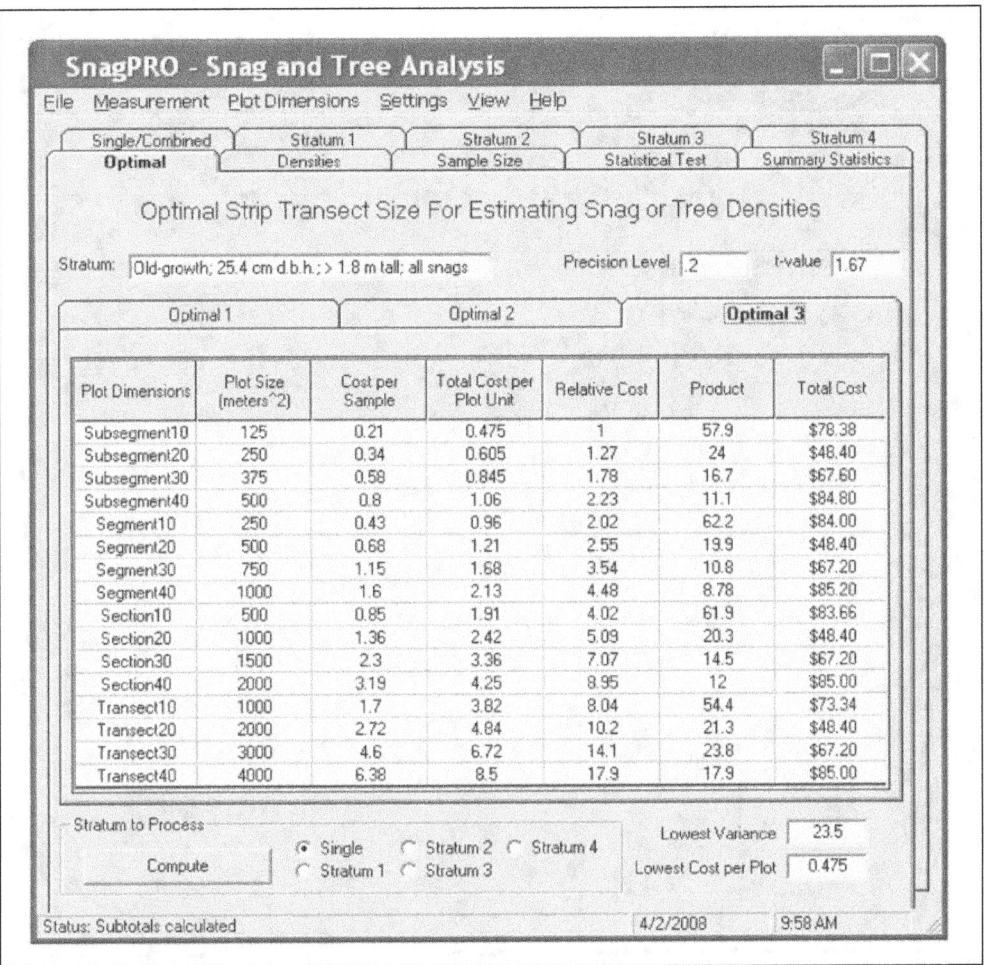

Figure 12—Optimal 3 page: third of three optimal pages showing cost per sample, total cost per plot unit, relative cost, product (cost x relative cost), and total cost for each plot size for both hard and soft snags in a single-stratum ponderosa pine landscape.

plots, 80 samples have been collected (even though Sample Size (Plots) shows 70). This number exceeds the minimum number of 60 samples required to meet the assumptions of normality.

On the **Optimal 3** page (fig. 12), examine the **Total Cost** for Subsegment20 plots and repeat steps described above for Segment20 plots. Lowest cost is the same as for the other width 20 plots ($48.40). To check for the independence of these plots, repeat steps described above for Segment20 plots. Results for independence show that Subsegment20 plots may be considered independent (r = 0.11 and r^2 = 0.01). Consequently, Subsegment20 plots are used for the remainder of the analyses and field sampling because this plot size appears best in meeting both objectives.

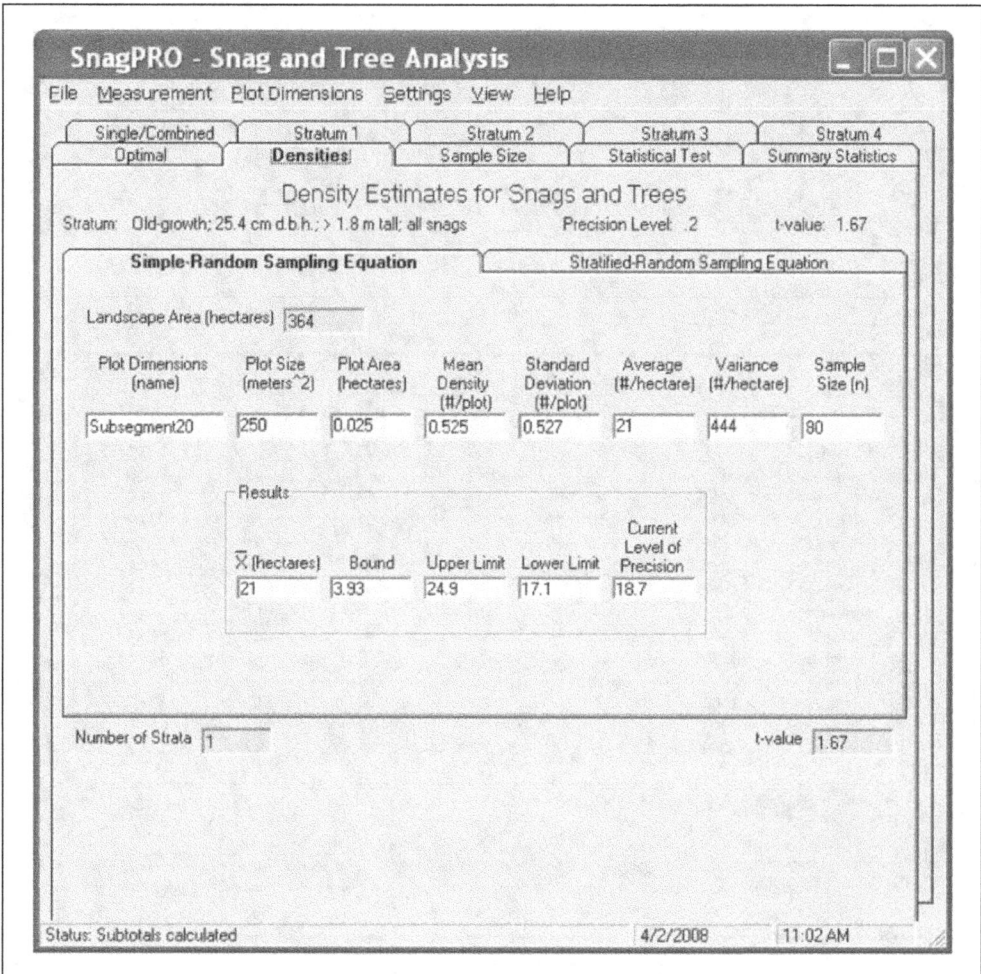

Figure 13—Densities page. Estimated density results using Subsegment20 plots for single-stratum ponderosa pine landscape. Results are for both hard and soft snags from the Tutorial_data_I_metric data set.

Density analysis—

First obtain a density estimate for snags in all decay classes because these are the data that currently fill the Optimal page. SnagPRO transfers the density statistics from the Optimal page to the Densities page based on which plot has the lowest total cost.

Go to **Densities | Simple-Random Sampling Equation** to obtain a density estimate for single-stratum landscapes. Check to ensure that **Subsegment20** is listed in the box labeled "Plot Dimensions (name)" to verify that the correct data have been transferred (fig. 13). Results show that this landscape supports 21 ± 3.93 snags per hectare. To determine the precision of your estimate, the bound is divided by the mean. For this example, the bound 3.93 is divided by the mean of 21, and then multiplied by 100. The result is 18.7. This indicates a 90-percent probability that the estimated mean density is within 18.7 percent of the true mean.

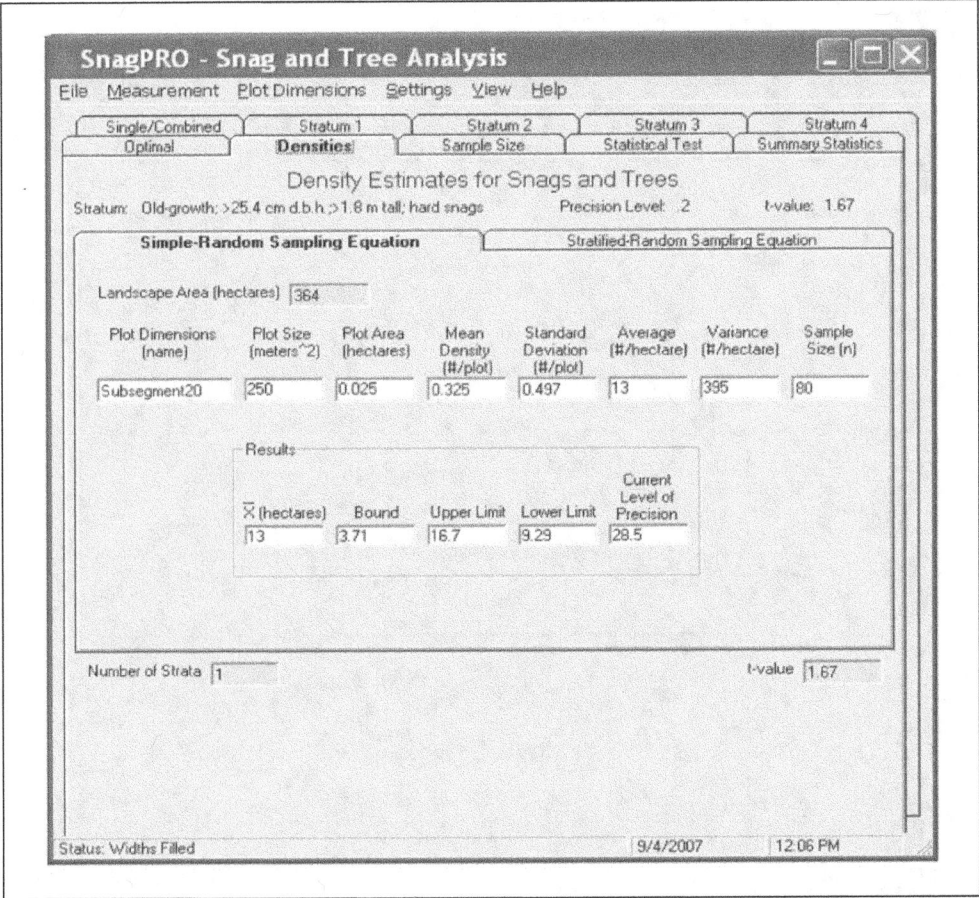

Figure 14—Densities page. Estimated density results using Subsegment20 plots for single-stratum ponderosa pine landscape. Optimal plot size was overridden by selecting Segment20 plots from the Optimal Selection on the Settings menu. Results are for hard snags from the Tutorial_data_I_metric data set.

Now obtain the density results for hard snags. Based on the previous analysis of hard snags, the lowest total cost comes with the Transect20 plots. However, it was determined that Subsegment20 plots would likely be best for both categories of snags. Consequently, the default Optimal plot selection needs to be overridden. To do this, follow these steps:

1. Go to the **Single/Combined** page.
2. Rerun the **Multiple** formula just for hard snags (Decay Class = **3**).
3. Go to **Settings | Optimal Selection**, and click on **Single Stratum**.
4. Select **Subsegment20** instead of Automatic.
5. Switch to **Optimal**, and click **Compute** in the lower left-hand corner.

Next, switch back to the **Densities** page (fig. 14). Results show that data for Subsegment20 plots have been transferred and that there are an estimated 13 ± 3.71 hard snags per hectare on this landscape. The current level of precision is 28.5 percent, which is less precise than the targeted goal.

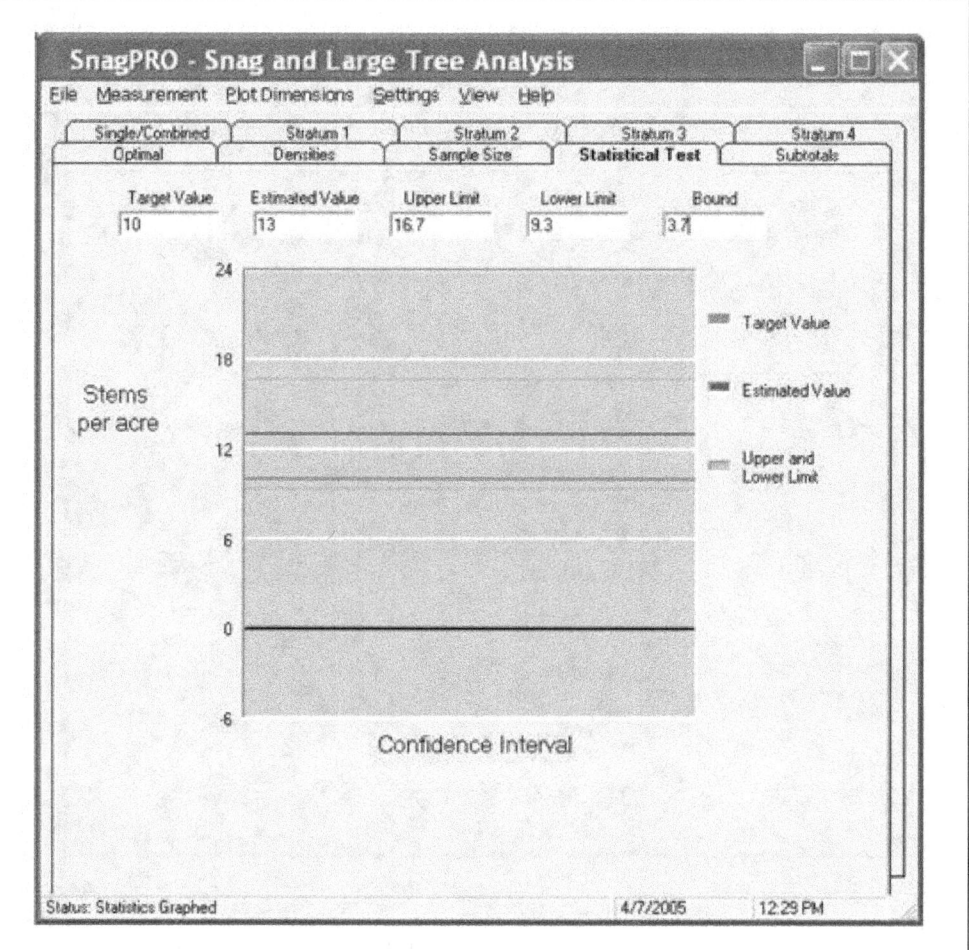

The graph shows that the line representing the target density for snags falls just within the boundaries of the upper and lower limits of the estimated density.

Figure 15—Statistical Test page. Graph depicting test for significant difference between estimated and targeted densities of qualifying hard snags in single-stratum ponderosa pine landscape. Results are from Tutorial_data_I_metric data set.

Compare to target density—

Assume that you have finished sampling and want to test whether the estimated density of qualifying snags meets the targeted density of 10 hard snags per hectare reported in the forest plan. Go to **Statistical Test** page to conduct the test, using the following steps:

1. Affirm the null hypothesis for this test: Ho: There is no difference between the estimated and the targeted hard snag densities.
2. Enter the targeted density of "10" into the shaded box labeled Target Value.
3. Enter the estimated snag density of "13" snags per hectare into the shaded box labeled Estimated Value.
4. Enter the estimated Bound of "3.7" for a 90-percent confidence interval.

Results are automatically plotted as a graph (fig. 15). The graph shows that the line representing the target density for snags falls just within the boundaries of the upper and lower limits of the estimated density. Consequently, the null hypothesis of "no difference between the estimated and targeted snag densities" is not rejected. The result indicates a 90-percent probability that the snag density on this landscape meets forest plan guidelines.

Cavity analysis—

To conduct the cavity analysis, return to the **Single/Combined** page. The cavity use codes are based on definitions described in appendix 2. To calculate the percentage of snags containing new cavities, follow these steps:

1. Click **Cavity** in the bottom-right corner of the **Single/Combined** page.
2. Enter "25.4" for the D.b.h. message box.
3. Enter "1.8" for Height.
4. Enter "5" for Decay Class.
5. Enter "9999" when prompted for any species to exclude (allows all species).
6. Enter "1" for Cavity Code (new cavity) (see app. 2).

Results show that of 48 available snags, 4 contained a new cavity. That is, 8 percent of the snags surveyed showed new signs of nesting. Note that several snags were excluded from the analysis because it was not possible to view the entire snag for signs of cavities, owing to its height or vegetation obstructing the view. In these cases, no value was placed in the cell in the Cavity column.

Conclusions for single stratum—

From this analysis, we may conclude:

- The estimated density of hard snags (13 ± 3.71 snags per hectare) on this landscape meets or exceeds the targeted densities listed in the forest plan (10 snags per hectare).
- The goal of obtaining an estimate of hard snags within 20 percent of the true mean, however, has not been achieved. To obtain this desired level of precision would require 83 additional plots. This translates to about 10 additional 100-m transects of 12.5-m subsegments.
- To save time in the field, distances will no longer be measured with a tape, but instead estimated by pacing because the plot width has been selected. Borderline cases, however, will continue to be measured.
- Snags in all decay classes averaged about 21 snags (± 3.93) per hectare.
- About 8 percent of all snags exhibit signs of recent use for nesting.

Example 2: Density Analysis for Subwatershed With Multiple Strata Using English Units

Background information—

To conduct forestwide compliance monitoring, a snag survey must be done on a representative subwatershed to determine if management activities have maintained designated snag densities for woodpeckers and other cavity-nesting species. Stands to be monitored are dominated by Douglas-fir/western hemlock communities. Owing to limited resources, monitoring will focus on whether the subwatershed meets forest plan standards for hard snags. However, data on snags for all decay classes will be collected if this does not substantially increase sampling effort.

Subwatershed stratification—

Aerial photographs show that the subwatershed is highly fragmented, and geospatial data verify that clearcutting has been the primary method of timber harvest. Ten years ago, a retention program was initiated for snags ≥18 in d.b.h., at least 20 ft tall, and in the decay classes I through III (Cline and others 1980). Owing to the timber harvest techniques used and the recent initiation of the snag retention program, snag densities are anticipated to be low in second-growth and most clearcut stands. In the old-growth stands, high densities of snags are anticipated.

Based on these expected differences, two strata may be sufficient: old-growth stands and a combined stratum of second-growth and clearcut stands. A thorough ground check, however, suggests that combining the second-growth and clearcut stands may not be feasible because the older clearcut stands have a dense understory that obstructs viewing. Stands that were clearcut >10 years ago are placed in their own stratum labeled "second growth." All clearcut stands harvested within the past 10 years are placed in a stratum labeled "clearcut."

Three strata have been delineated: clearcut, second growth, and old growth. Make a field map of the stand polygons assigned to each stratum. Attribute each stand with its number of acres and the total acres for that stratum within the entire subwatershed. Strata 1, 2, and 3 have 1,759, 1,381, and 1,243 acres, respectively, for a total of 4,383 acres. Spend a day in the field, validating that each stand has been placed in the proper stratum.

Pilot survey—

Although topography of the subwatershed ranges from flat benches to steep (>100 percent) slopes, clearcut harvest has occurred mostly in flat areas. Visibility within the clearcut stratum is unobstructed, travel is easy, and snag densities appear low. Therefore, preselect the widest plot width—132 ft—to maximize sampling efficiency.

A preliminary review of the second-growth stands, however, reveals difficult travel conditions and low visibility. Few, if any, snags are expected in these stands because they were harvested before a snag retention policy was adopted. Consequently, choose a narrower plot—66 ft—to ensure that snags are not missed because of viewing obstructions.

Snag densities within the old growth are highly variable. Thus, the best choice for plot width is not apparent. Visibility averages about 49.5 feet, and travel is moderate to difficult, owing to a large volume of logs and dense patches of understory trees and shrubs. Thus, plots 99-ft wide are chosen, allowing a formal optimal plot size analysis to be conducted for the stratum.

Across the watershed, five stands of each stratum are randomly selected in which two 400-ft-long transects are established. Starting points for each transect are selected by placing a grid over each stand and then randomly choosing a grid intersection for the starting point (fig. 1). The compass direction also is randomly determined.

Each transect is assigned a unique numeric identifier, and divided into eight 50-ft subsegments, numbered 1 through 8. The bounce-back method is used for any transects running into the stand boundaries (fig. 4). In each subsegment, all snags of interest are tallied from the center line: 66 ft for stratum 1; 33 ft for stratum 2; and 49.5 ft for stratum 3.

Data entry—

Data for all strata within this subwatershed are found in Snag_Tutorial_Data, on the Tutorial_data_II_English page, found at the PNW Web site at http://www.fs.fed.us/pnw/publications/tools-databases.shtml. Data in this MS Excel spreadsheet are for 30 transects, each divided into eight subsegments. Data are in the same format as the field form (fig. 5), with one exception. An additional column, Plot width, was added on the field form to help track sampling within each stratum. This extraneous column is not included in the CSV import file, however, because its header information is not recognized by SnagPRO.

Consecutive subsegments—

Before starting the analysis, sort transects and subsegments in ascending order to verify that there are eight subsegments for each transect. To do this, go to the menu, **Data | Sort**, and select **ascending** for both **Sort By** and **Then By**. Make sure that eight subsegment lengths are entered for each transect, and that the beginning subsegment of each transect is numbered "1."

Saving as a CSV file—

SnagPRO imports only CSV files. To create a CSV file, follow these steps:

1. Activate the **Tutorial_data_II_English** sheet by clicking anywhere on the sheet.
2. Select **File | Save As**.
3. Click **Save as Type** at the bottom of the Save As message box.
4. Select CSV (comma delimited) (*.**csv**).
5. Assign a new file name in the file name box.
6. Click **Save**. When saved as a CSV file, only the active sheet is retained. Saving the file with a different name keeps the original file intact.

Importing to SnagPRO—

Import the CSV file of snag data using these steps:

1. Launch SnagPRO by double-clicking on the desktop icon or the executable file— **SnagPRO.exe**.
2. Click **Snags or Trees**.
3. Go to **Measurement**, and click **English**.
4. Go to **File | Open**. In the message box "Look in," browse to the folder containing the CSV data and select the file name.

This should successfully import the CSV file. Additional columns have been added to your file:

- The Segment and Section columns were inserted between Transect and Subsegment.
- Width33, Width66, Width99, and Width132 columns have been added.

SnagPRO combined consecutive subsegments (50-ft lengths) into segments (100-ft lengths), and segments into sections (200-ft lengths). The Width columns are populated after you select a formula (see below).

Formula entry—

Create the formulas so SnagPRO places the correct values into the Width columns. These formulas determine which snags are included in the current analysis.

First obtain estimates of hard snags only. To do this, locate and click on the **Single/Combined** page. Then click the **Multiple** button to have SnagPRO include multiple species in the analysis. Several input boxes will then appear. To create the correct formula, based on survey objectives, enter:

- "18" for D.b.h.
- "20" for Height.
- "3" for Decay Class (hard snags based on Cline and others [1980]).
- "9999" for Species (all snag species are included).

SnagPRO evaluates each snag in each Width column for the criteria listed above plus its distance from the centerline. For snags meeting all criteria, a value of "1" is placed in the cell; otherwise, the cell receives a "0." After the formulas have been created, SnagPRO will sort the data by stratum and place the appropriate data on each stratum page.

Analyzing by plot size—
SnagPRO now calculates averages and standard deviations for each plot size, transferring the results to the Optimal pages. First, review General Cost per Sample Guidelines under the **View** menu to select one of the six cost categories that best applies to your forest conditions (see the "Estimating Costs" section and table 3 for details).

Choose **Code 1** for stratum 1 because the clearcut harvesting resulted in open conditions and low snag densities. Choose **Code 5** in stratum 2 because travel conditions are difficult, visibility is limited, and snag densities are low. Choose **Code 6** for the stratum 3 because of difficult travel conditions, limited visibility, and higher snag densities.

To sum and subtotal the values for each plot size in stratum 1:
- Click the **Optimal** tab.
- Go to **Stratum to Process.**
- Select **Stratum 1**.
- Click **Compute**.

A series of message boxes will appear. Enter:
- "3" into the Number of Strata message box.
- "1" into the General Cost per Sample box (this is the code we chose for stratum 1).
- "1759" for Stratum 1 Size.
- "1381" for Stratum 2 Size.
- "1243" for Stratum 3 Size.

Stratum 1 analysis—
The results on the Optimal page are for hard snags in stratum 1. Write this description in the Stratum box at the top of the page. On the Optimal 1 page (fig. 16), the narrower plots (Width33 and Width66) have zeros for Mean Density (#/plot) because only one qualifying snag was found in stratum 1, at a distance of 46 ft from the centerline (shown on the Summary Statistics page). Mean Density (#/acre) for the wider plots is estimated to be about 0.1 snag per acre.

On the Optimal 3 page, the Transect99 plots have the lowest Total Cost value ($2,491.68), making this the optimal plot size. This excludes plots without snags

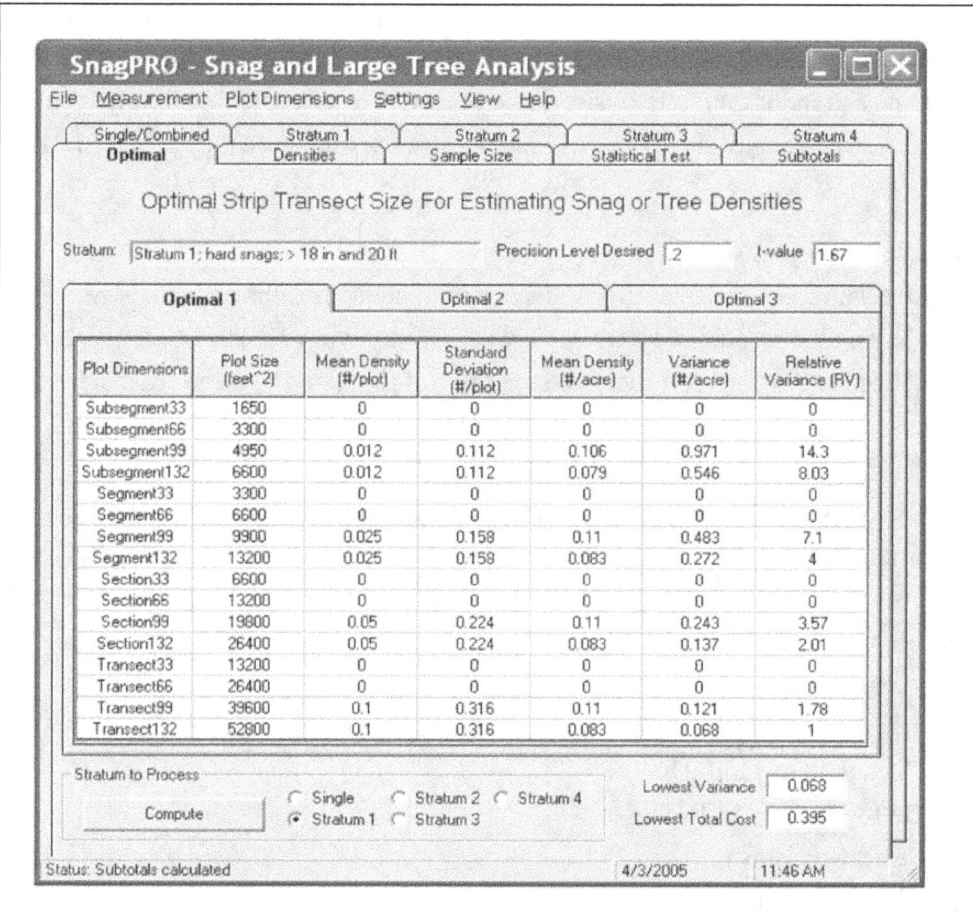

Figure 16—Optimal 1 page: first of three optimal pages showing size (m^2), mean, standard deviation, variance, and relative variance for each plot size for hard snags in a stratified Douglas-fir/western hemlock forest landscape. No qualifying snags were found in the two narrowest plots. Therefore, these cells only contain "0."

Total Cost is high for the nonstratified landscape with 696 plots required; if we analyze strata, the sample size required would be substantially lower.

in them. The Total Cost is extremely high within this stratum, because SnagPRO is currently treating it as a nonstratified landscape and the estimated sample size required within this stratum is 696 plots (shown on the Optimal 2 page). If we analyze as strata within a subwatershed, however, the sample size required would be substantially lower.

Stratum 2—

To sum and subtotal the values for each plot size in stratum 2:

- Click the **Optimal** tab.
- Go to **Stratum to Process**.
- Select **Stratum 2**.
- Click **Compute**.

Enter "5" when asked for the General Cost per Sample code. Note on the Stratum 2 page that, as in stratum 1, only one snag was encountered. The decay class for this snag, however, was "4," which makes it a soft snag, therefore not qualifying in this analysis and making the hard snag density equal to zero.

Stratum 3—

To sum and subtotal the values for each plot size in stratum 3:

- Click the **Optimal** tab.
- Go to **Stratum to Process**.
- Select **Stratum 3**.
- Click **Compute**.

Enter "6" when asked for the General Cost per Sample code. In contrast to the previous analyses, many hard snags were encountered in stratum 3.

Note the estimated mean snag densities in each of the plot sizes on the Optimal 1 page. The three narrowest plots are in close agreement with each other (3.52 to 3.8 snags per acre), whereas for plots that are 132 ft wide, the density drops considerably, to 2.6 snags per acre. In this situation, it is best to select one of the narrower plots, because the lower density may have been caused by observers "missing" some of the snags on the outer boundaries of plots.

Looking at the Optimal 2 page for stratum 3, note that Transect66 plots require the lowest number of samples (23.7 plots), but when these samples are converted to acres, the Section66 plots have the minimum number of acres (13.9 acres), suggesting these as the better plot size.

Skim the values listed in the Product column on the Optimal 3 page. When Relative Cost is multiplied by the Relative Variance, we find the Section66 plots have the lowest product (14.5) of all plot sizes. Consequently, based on Wiegert's (1962) method, this is the optimal plot size for sampling snags in this forest stratum.

Look at Total Cost to see if total costs support the values found in the Product column. If so, then this plot size would minimize our costs ($182) and achieve the desired precision. Additionally, we would not jeopardize accuracy by sampling beyond the point of clear visibility from the centerline. Section66 plots, therefore, seem to be the optimal plot size for use within stratum 3, but are these plots independent?

To test for independence, switch to the **Summary Statistics** page and run the serial correlation test for Section66 plots in stratum 3. To do this:

1. Click on the **Correlation** button in the bottom-right corner of the screen.
2. Enter "Section" when the first message box appears labeled "Correlation Length."
3. Enter "66" into the Correlation Width box.

The message box displays the correlation coefficient ($r = 0.0$) and coefficient of determination ($r^2 = 0.0$). The extremely low r^2 value (0.0) verifies that adjacent Section66 plots appear to be independent sampling units. Therefore, this plot size is used for the remainder of the analyses.

Stratified density analysis—

To obtain an estimate of the required sample size for this subwatershed, we first need an estimate of the stratified mean density to enter in the sample size equation. To do this:

- Click on the **Densities** page.
- Activate the **Stratified-Random Sampling Equation** page.
- Click the **Calculate Stratified Values** button, toward the bottom of the page.

SnagPRO transfers all statistics to the Densities page and fills in the Stratum Sizes (acres) with previous entries. If necessary, values in the shaded boxes can be changed. It is estimated that there are 1.12 hard snags (± 0.334) per acre in this subwatershed (fig. 17) at a 29.8 percent level of precision. Results indicate that the estimated hard snag density for this subwatershed is within 29.8 percent of the true mean under a 90-percent confidence interval, which is not as precise as desired.

Sample size determination—

The next step is to determine the sample size needed to achieve the desired precision. Sample sizes for stratified subwatersheds are calculated on the Sample Size page, so activate this page. SnagPRO transferred the statistics to the Sample Size page once the stratified density estimate was calculated.

In the lower portion of the Sample Size page (fig. 18), see the output from two sample size equations—Optimal Allocation and Proportional Allocation. The Optimal allocation method incorporates the strata variances into its calculations, estimating that 55.2 samples are required to obtain a stratified mean within 20 percent of the true mean 90 percent of the time. These 55 samples are then divided among the three strata: 7.61 plots in stratum 1 (clearcuts), no plots in stratum 2 (second growth), and 47.6 plots in stratum 3 (old growth). With rounding, this results in 56 total samples required: 8 in stratum 1 and 48 in stratum 3.

To the right of the page is the heading Proportional Allocation. This method uses the overall variance of the subwatershed to allocate the samples, based on the

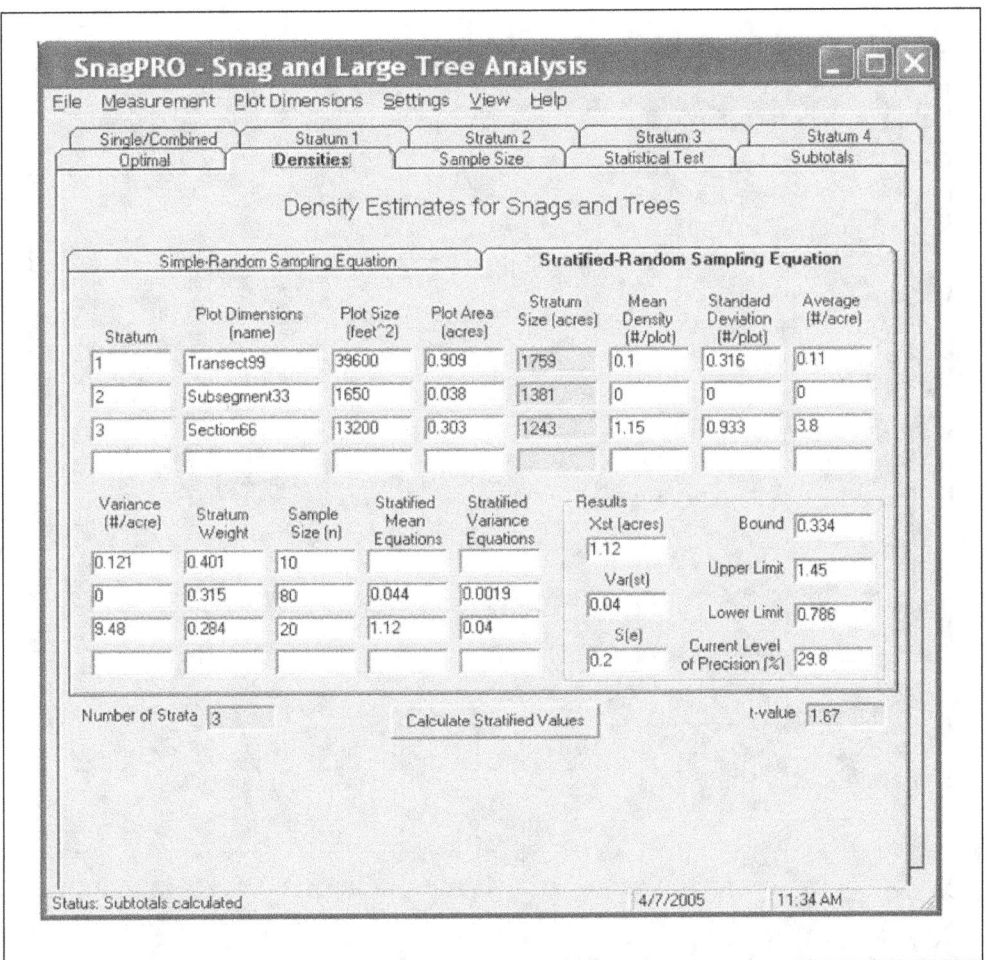

Figure 17—Stratified mean density estimate with a 90-percent confidence interval for qualifying hard snags for the Douglas-fir/western hemlock landscape. Data are from page labeled "Tutorial_data_II_ English" in the Snag_Tutorial_Data file.

relative size of each stratum. The results state that 153 samples are needed to obtain the same precision (20 percent of the true mean 90 percent of the time), which, after rounding to whole numbers for each stratum, yields 61 plots in stratum 1, 48 plots in stratum 2, and 44 plots in stratum 3.

Both sample size equations are in agreement regarding the number of samples needed for stratum 3. There are large discrepancies however, for stratum 1 and stratum 2. The optimal method suggests focusing most of the effort in stratum 3 (n = 47.6), which has the largest variance relative to the other strata. The optimal method recommends no samples in stratum 2, whereas the proportional method suggests 48.2 sample plots.

In this situation, it is best to follow the numbers suggested by the optimal allocation equation. That is, no additional sampling is needed within strata 1 and 2, unless it is suspected that encountering such low snag numbers within these

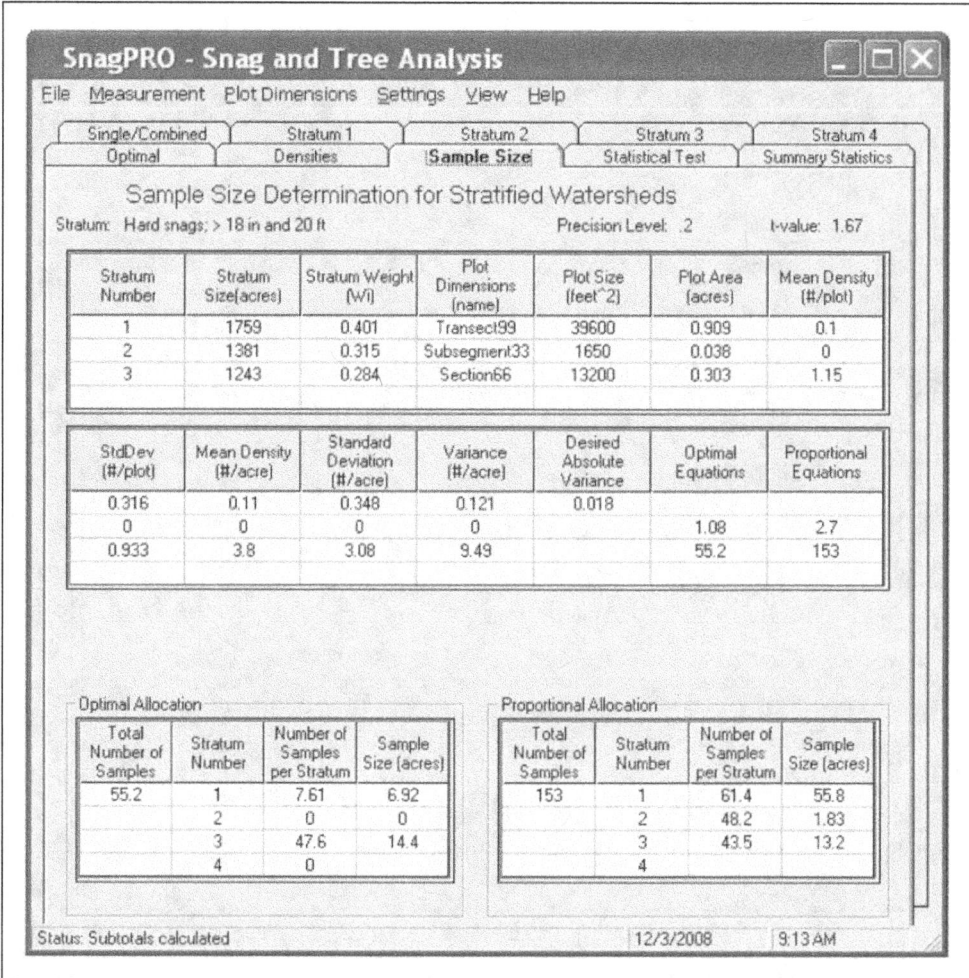

Figure 18—Sample size page. Optimal and proportional sample size calculations for sampling hard snags in each of three strata on the Douglas-fir/western hemlock landscape. Data are from page labeled 'Tutorial_data_II_English' in the file named Snag_Tutorial_Data file.

As additional data are collected, entered, and analyzed, the variances and thus the required sample size may change within a stratum.

stands for the pilot sample was an inaccurate representation of the conditions. Instead, focus sampling effort in stratum 3 by surveying 14 additional transects (400-ft lengths) to obtain 28 additional Section66 plots. Sampling will proceed more quickly now that the optimal plot width has been identified. This eliminates the need to measure all the distances of snags from the centerline. After completion of these 28 plots, the estimated sample size requirement of 48 will have been met. Data can then be analyzed to determine whether to continue sampling to increase precision, or to stop because precision meets the sampling objectives.

Again, remember that the sample size equations simply provide an estimate of the number of samples required, given current sample data. As additional data are collected, entered, and analyzed, the variances and thus the required sample size may change within a stratum. This possibility increases if the pilot sample data are a poor representation of the variation within a stratum. Consequently, the best way to avoid oversampling (where large sample sizes are required) is to continually enter data in SnagPRO and periodically calculate a mean density and its bound to determine the current precision. See the discussion of sample size determination in the "SnagPRO Analysis" section for a description of the advantages and disadvantages of optimal and proportional allocation methods for determining sample size.

Compare to target density—

Assume that 60 samples have been collected, and thus it is appropriate to test whether the estimated density of snags meets the targeted density identified in the forest plan. The bound on the density estimate for the 90-percent confidence interval has already been calculated, which is 1.12 ± 0.334 target snags per acre (see Data Sheet page). Now activate the page labeled **Statistical Test** by clicking on this tab. To conduct the test, follow these steps:

1. The analysis is based on the null hypothesis: H_0: There is no difference between the estimated and the targeted hard snag densities.
2. Assume that the target density for hard snags in this subwatershed is "1.51" snags per acre. Enter this value in the shaded Target Value box.
3. Enter the estimated snag density of "1.12" snags per acre into the shaded Estimated Value box.
4. Enter the estimated Bound for a 90-percent confidence interval: "0.334."

Once the necessary information has been entered onto the Statistical Test page, a graph depicting the results is automatically created (fig. 19). The graph shows that the line representing the target density for snags does not overlap the upper and lower limits of the estimated density. Consequently, the null hypothesis of no difference between the estimated and targeted snag densities is rejected. These test results, however, are inconclusive until we have attained our desired level of precision. The 14 additional transects (which contain 28 section samples) in stratum 3 should meet these requirements. Data from the additional samples can then be considered and new results entered on the Statistical Test page.

Conclusions for multiple strata—

- Results suggest that the estimated density of hard snags (1.12 ± 0.334 snags per acre) on this landscape fails to meet the targeted densities listed in the forest plan (1.51 snags per acre).
- Results also indicate that snags needed to sustain woodpecker populations may be inadequate in this subwatershed, because large portions of the subwatershed do not contain hard snags. This is a problem because woodpeckers are territorial.

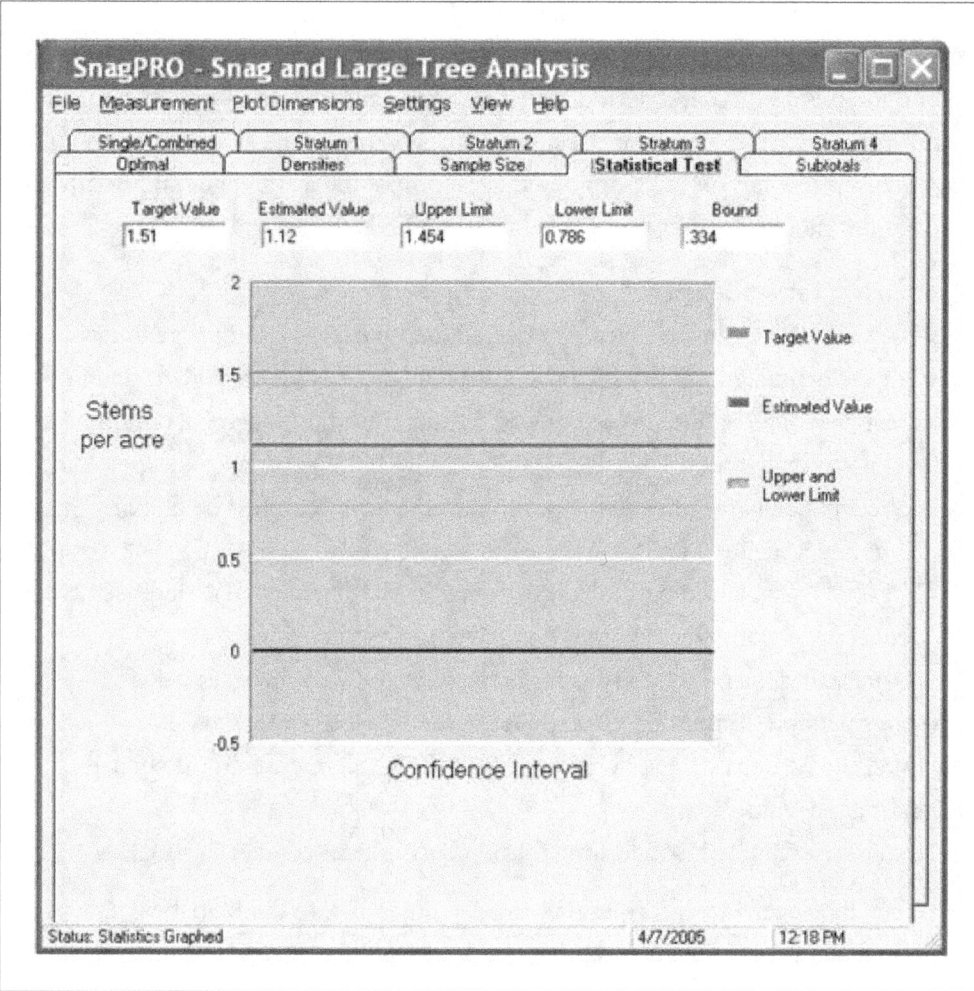

Figure 19—Statistical test page. Graph depicting test for significant difference between estimated and targeted densities of qualifying snags on Douglas-fir/western hemlock landscape. Input data are from figure 17.

- These tests are inconclusive, however, until we attain the specified level of precision.
- Snags in all decay classes averaged about 2.48 snags (± 0.64) per acre.

Management options include (1) continue sampling to increase the precision of estimates and to determine whether results of the analysis will change; (2) sample recent clearcut areas for the number and quality of retained snags; (3) increase snag retention efforts as part of timber harvest planning, layout, and implementation; and (4) initiate snag creation programs to increase the density and improve the distribution of snags in the subwatershed.

Acknowledgments

We thank Deb Hennessy, Amy Jacobs, and Christine Vojta for their careful reviews of our manuscript and for pilot testing the snag and tree portion of SnagPRO. Evelyn Bull, Trish Heekin, and Kim Mellen reviewed earlier versions of our manuscript. Kirk Steinhorst provided a thorough statistical review. Will Hutchinson, Christine Hunter, Phil Talbot, Kris Allison, Klaus Rossini, Ian Cole, and Adam Messer assisted in data collection. Jennifer Boyd edited the manuscript and produced the final figures. Funding was provided by the Pacific Northwest Region and the Washington office of the USDA Forest Service. Lisa Norris, Richard Holthausen, and Christina Vojta were instrumental in securing funds and in providing helpful direction regarding management applications.

Metric Equivalents

When you know:	Multiply by:	To find:
Inches (in)	2.54	Centimeters (cm)
Feet (ft)	0.305	Meters (m)
Acres	0.405	Hectares (ha)

Literature Cited

Bate, L.J. 1995. Monitoring woodpecker abundance and habitat in the central Oregon Cascades. Moscow, ID: University of Idaho. 116 p. M.S. thesis.

Bate, L.J.; Garton, E.O.; Wisdom, M.J. 1999. Estimating snag and large tree densities and distributions on a landscape for wildlife management. Gen. Tech. Rep. PNW-425. Portland, OR: U.S. Department of Agriculture, Forest Service, Pacific Northwest Research Station. 76 p.

Bate, L.J.; Torgersen, T.R.; Wisdom, M.J.; Garton, E.O.; Clabough, S.C. 2008. Log sampling methods and software for stand and landscape analyses. Gen. Tech. Rep. PNW-746. Portland, OR: U.S. Department of Agriculture, Forest Service, Pacific Northwest Research Station. 93 p.

Bate, L.J.; Wisdom, M.J.; Wales, B.C. 2007. Snag densities in relation to human access and associated management factors in forests of northeastern Oregon, USA. Landscape and Urban Planning. 80: 278-291.

Beebe, S.B. 1974. Relationships between insectivorous hole-nesting birds and forest management. New Haven, CT: Yale University, School of Forestry and Environmental Studies. 49 p.

Betts, B.J. 1998. Roosts used by maternity colonies of silver-haired bats in northeastern Oregon. Journal of Mammology. 79(2): 643-650.

Brown, R.E., tech. ed. 1985. Management of wildlife and fish habitats in forests of western Oregon and Washington. R6-F&WL-192-1985. Portland, OR: U.S. Department of Agriculture, Forest Service, Pacific Northwest Region. 332 p.

Bull, E.L.; Carter, B.; Henjum, M.; Holthausen, R.; Johnson, J.; Mellen, K. 1991. Monitoring protocol—October 1991. Protocol for monitoring woodpeckers and snags in the Pacific Northwest Region of U.S. Forest Service. 8 p. Unpublished report. On file with: U.S. Department of Agriculture, Forest Service, Pacific Northwest Research Station, Forestry and Range Sciences Laboratory, 1401 Gekeler Lane, La Grande, OR 97850.

Bull, E.L.; Holthausen, R.S. 1993. Habitat use and management of pileated woodpeckers in northeastern Oregon. Journal of Wildlife Management. 57: 335-345.

Bull, E.L.; Holthausen, R.S.; Marx, D.B. 1990. How to determine snag density. Western Journal of Applied Forestry. 5(2): 56-58.

Bull, E.L.; Parks, C.G.; Torgersen, T.R. 1997. Trees and logs important to wildlife in the Interior Columbia River basin. Gen. Tech. Rep. PNW-391. Portland, OR: U.S. Department of Agriculture, Forest Service, Pacific Northwest Research Station. 55 p.

Bull, E.L.; Peterson, S.R.; Thomas, J.W. 1986. Resource partitioning among woodpeckers in northeastern Oregon. Res. Note. PNW-444. Portland, OR: U.S. Department of Agriculture, Forest Service, Pacific Northwest Forest and Range Experiment Station. 19 p.

Bütler, R.; Schlaepfer, R. 2004. Spruce snag quantification by coupling colour infrared aerial photos and a GIS. Forest Ecology and Management. 195: 325-339.

Campbell, L.A.; Hallett, J.G.; O'Connell, M.A. 1996. Conservation of bats in managed forests: use of roosts by *Lasionycteris noctivagans*. Journal of Mammalogy. 77: 976-984.

Caton, E. 1996. Effects of fire and salvage-logging on a cavity-nesting bird community in northwestern Montana. Missoula, MT: University of Montana. 115 p. Ph.D. dissertation.

Cline, S.P.; Berg, A.B.; Wight, H.M. 1980. Snag characteristics and dynamics in Douglas-fir forests, western Oregon. Journal of Wildlife Management. 44(4): 773-786.

Cochran, W.G. 1977. Sampling techniques. 3rd ed. New York: John Wiley and Sons. 428 p.

Dickson, J.G.; Conner, R.N.; Williamson, J.H. 1983. Snag retention increases bird use of a clear cut. Journal of Wildlife Management. 47(3): 799-804.

Dixon, R. 1995. Ecology of white-headed woodpeckers in the central Oregon Cascades. Moscow, ID: University of Idaho. 148 p. M.S. thesis.

Ducey, M.J.; Jordan, G.J.; Gove, J.H.; Valentine, H.T. 2002. A practical modification of horizontal line sampling for snag and cavity tree inventory. Canadian Journal of Forest Research. 32: 1217-1224.

Ffolliott, P.F. 1983. Implications of snag policies on management of southwestern ponderosa pine forests. In: Davis, J.W.; Goodwin, G.A.; Ockenfels, R.A., tech. ed. Snag habitat management symposium. Gen. Tech. Rep. RM-99. Flagstaff, AZ: U.S. Department of Agriculture, Forest Service, Rocky Mountain Forest and Range Experiment Station: 28-32.

Hann, W.J.; Jones, J.L.; Karl, M.G.; Hessburg, P.F.; Keane, R.E.; Long, D.G.; Menakis, J.P.; McNicoll, C.H.; Leonard, S.G.; Gravenmier, R.A.; Smith, B.G. 1997. Landscape dynamics of the basin. In: Quigley, T.M.; Arbelbide, S.J., tech. eds. An assessment of ecosystem components in the interior Columbia basin and portions of the Klamath and Great Basins. Gen. Tech. Rep. PNW-405. Portland, OR: U.S. Department of Agriculture, Forest Service, Pacific Northwest Research Station: 334-1056.

Harmon, M.E.; Sexton, J. 1996. Guidelines for measurements of woody detritus in forest ecosystems. Publ. No. 20. Seattle, WA: U.S. Long-Term Ecological Research (LTER) Network Office, University of Washington. 73 p.

Hope, S.; McComb, W.C. 1994. Perceptions of implementing and monitoring wildlife tree prescriptions on national forests in western Washington and Oregon. Wildlife Society Bulletin. 22: 383-393.

Hurlbert, S.H. 1984. Pseudoreplication and the design of ecological field experiments. Ecological Monographs. 54(2): 187-211.

Husch, T.; Beers, W.; Kershaw, J. 1972. Forest mensuration. 2nd ed. New York: The Ronald Press Company. 410 p.

Kenning, R.; Ducey, M.; Brisette, J.; Gove, J. 2005. Field efficiency and bias of snag inventory methods. Canadian Journal of Forest Research: 35(12): 2900-2910.

Krebs, C.J. 1989. Ecological methodology. New York: Harper Collins Publishers, Inc. 654 p.

Laudenslayer, W.F., Jr. 2002. Cavity-nesting bird use of snags in eastside pine forests of northeastern California. Gen. Tech. Rep. PSW-181. Fresno, CA: U.S. Department of Agriculture, Forest Service, Pacific Southwest Research Station: 223-236.

Ligon, J.D. 1973. Foraging behavior of the white-headed woodpecker in Idaho. Auk. 90: 862-869.

Mariani, J.M.; Manuwal, D.A. 1990. Factors influencing brown creeper (*Certhia americana*) abundance patterns in the southern Washington Cascade Range. Studies in Avian Biology. 13: 53-57.

Mellen, K.; Marcot, B.G.; Ohmann, J.L.; Waddell, K.; Livingston, S.A.; Willhite, E.A.; Hostetler, B.B.; Ogden, C.; Dreisbach, T. 2006. DecAID, the decayed wood advisor for managing snags, partially dead trees, and down wood for biodiversity in forests of Washington and Oregon. Version 2.0. Portland, OR: USDA Forest Service, Pacific Northwest Region and Pacific Northwest Research Station; USDI Fish and Wildlife Service, Oregon State Office. http://wwwnotes.fs.fed.us:81/pnw/DecAID/DecAID.nsf. (April 4, 2008).

Morrison, M.L.; Dedon, M.F.; Raphael, M.G.; Yoder-Williams, M.P. 1986. Snag requirements of cavity-nesting birds: Are USDA Forest Service guidelines being met? Western Journal of Applied Forestry. 1: 38-40.

Ormsbee, P.C.; McComb, W.C. 1998. Selection of day roosts by female longlegged myotis in the central Oregon Cascade Range. Journal of Wildlife Management. 62(2): 596-603.

Otvos, I.S. 1979. The effects of insectivorous bird activities in forest ecosystems: an evaluation. In: Dickson, J.G.; Connor, R.N.; Fleet, R.R. [and others], eds. The role of insectivorous birds in forest ecosystems. New York: Academic Press: 341-374.

Parks, C.G.; Bull, E.L.; Torgersen, T.R. 1997. Field guide for the identification of snags and logs in the interior Columbia River basin. Gen. Tech. Rep. PNW-390. Portland, OR: U.S. Department Agriculture, Forest Service, Pacific Northwest Research Station. 40 p.

Quigley, T.M.; Haynes, R.W.; Graham, R.T., tech. eds. 1996. Integrated scientific assessment for ecosystem management in the interior Columbia basin and portions of the Klamath and Great Basins. Gen. Tech. Rep. PNW-382. Portland, OR: U.S. Department of Agriculture, Forest Service, Pacific Northwest Research Station. 303 p.

Rose, C.L.; Marcot, B.G.; Mellen, T.K.; Ohmann, J.L.; Waddell, K.L.; Lindley, D.L.; Schreiber, B. 2001. Decaying wood in Pacific Northwest forests: concepts and tools for habitat management. In: Johnson, D.H.; O'Neil, T.A., eds. Wildlife-habitat relationships in Oregon and Washington. Corvallis, OR: Oregon State University Press: 580-623. http://www.nwhi.org/inc/data/GISdata/docs/chapter24.pdf. (April 2007)

Saab, V.; Dudley, J. 1998. Responses of cavity-nesting birds to stand-replacement fire and salvage logging in ponderosa pine/Douglas-fir forests of southwestern Idaho. Res. Pap. RMRS-11. Ogden, UT: U.S. Department of Agriculture, Forest Service, Rocky Mountain Research Station. 17 p.

Sokal, R.R.; Rohlf, F.J. 1981. Biometry. New York: W.H. Freeman and Company. 859 p.

Styskel, E.W. 1983. Problems in snag management implementation–a case study. In: Snag habitat management: proceedings of the symposium. Gen. Tech. Rep. RM-99. Fort Collins, CO: U.S. Department of Agriculture, Forest Service, Rocky Mountain Forest and Range Experiment Station: 24-27.

Swihart, R.K.; Slade, N.A. 1985. Testing for independence of observations in animal movements. Ecology. 66(4): 1176-1184.

Thomas, J.W.; Anderson, R.G.; Maser, C.; Bull, E.L. 1979. Snags. In: Wildlife habitats in managed forests--the Blue Mountains of Oregon and Washington. Agric. Handb. 553. Washington, DC: U.S. Department of Agriculture: 60-77

U.S. Department of Agriculture, Forest Service. 1991. Field procedures guide: stand examination program. Portland, OR: U.S. Department of Agriculture, Forest Service, Pacific Northwest Region.

Wiegert, R.G. 1962. The selection of an optimum quadrat size for sampling the standing crop of grasses and forbs. Ecology. 43(1): 125-129.

Wisdom, M.J.; Bate, L.J. 2008. Snag density varies with intensity of timber harvest and human access. Forest Ecology and Management. 255(7): 2085-2093.

Appendix 1: General Snag and Tree Sampling Guidelines

1. Sampling objectives.
   a. What snag (tree) size(s) will be surveyed (diameter and height)?
   b. What condition (decay class) of snags (trees) will be surveyed?
   c. How will the data be used? Baseline data? Compliance data? This often dictates answers to the following questions.
   d. How precise does the estimate need to be?
   e. Is snag/tree species important? If so, why?
   f. Will signs of wildlife use be recorded (for example, woodpecker foraging, cavities?)?
   g. Are estimates for separate areas needed?
2. Landscape definition and selection.
   a. Define the landscape, or area of interest, by delineating the boundaries. This area is the sampling frame, within which a random sample is drawn for the purpose of making inferences to the entire area.
      3. Landscape stratification.
   a. Visit the survey area first, if it is unfamiliar, with a map delineating the boundaries. What differences/similarities are visible in regard to snag/tree abundance and/or vegetative structure across the landscape?
   b. Obtain reference maps for field use, such as geographic information system maps or U.S. Geological Survey orthoquad maps, or both. Always request metadata (data definitions) for the polygon data. Maps should display the following information:
      i. Road system with difference in road type and maintenance level displayed.
      ii. Stand, polygon, or vegetation units and their respective unique numeric identifiers.
      iii. Current seral stage of vegetation at a scale of 1:31,680 or better resolution. Keep in mind that scale is a ratio or fraction, so polygons mapped at 1:24,000 scale will appear larger than they do in the 1:31,680-scale map. This information may be on one or more maps.
   c. Query the polygon database for information about forest type (low versus high elevation, dry versus moist), management activities, seral stage, disturbance history (wind, fire, insects, and disease), and any other factors that may affect snag/tree abundance. Ensure that the report includes types of management activities, such as harvest method used, slash and burn prescriptions, thinning, and snag/tree retention.

d. Check the map and information from the polygon database for general agreement with features that can be viewed with aerial photographs of the area. The degree to which the map and database information appear similar to what is shown on the aerial photographs provides a good indication about how much field reconnaissance will be needed for accurate landscape stratification.

e. Revisit the survey area with the field maps. Plan to spend at least one day to validate the information on the map(s) and in the report from the query. Assign each polygon to a stratum. Estimate the number of acres (ha) within each polygon or stratum.

4. Establishing transects

a. There are two options for establishing transects: the single-stratum landscape method, and the stratified method. For the single-stratum landscape method, follow these steps to establish transects within a single polygon or a nonstratified landscape:

   i. Randomly place a grid over the area.

   ii. Randomly select 10 grid points for sampling.

   iii. Randomly select compass bearings for each of the 10 transect starting points.

b. For the stratified method on heterogeneous landscapes composed of numerous polygons or units, it may be more efficient to randomly select polygons for sampling. To do this:

   i. Select polygons for sampling by randomly picking polygon unit numbers from the complete list of polygons within that stratum.

   ii. Place a grid over the polygon.

   iii. Randomly pick two grid points within each polygon.

   iv. Randomly pick compass bearings for each point.

5. Plot size selection

a. Based on information gathered during the stratification process, it may be beneficial to preselect a plot size for sampling. Wide plots work best in areas of low snag densities, unlimited visibility, and easy travel conditions. Narrower plots (66 ft or 20 m wide) work best in areas of higher densities or clumped distributions or where visibility is limited. The smallest plots work best in extremely high-density areas.

b. Postpilot sampling plot size selection. In most forested conditions, the optimal plot size for sampling is unknown until the density and distribution of the snags or trees can be evaluated. In these situations:

   i. Use pilot sample data to determine which plot sizes minimize sampling effort to obtain your desired objectives. See "Optimal Plot Size Analysis" section for details.

   ii. Use optimal plot size for remainder of survey.

6. Field surveying techniques

   a. Use an engineer's surveying or measuring tape to establish transects, starting each transect from the randomly selected points (described above).

   b. Assign a unique numeric identifier to each transect, delineating the subsegment lengths (50 ft [or 12.5 m]) as you walk along the transect (400 ft or 100 m).

   c. Number each transect's subsegments 1 through 8.

   d. Conduct a complete count of all qualifying snags or trees out to 66 ft (20 m), using the tape as centerline. A snag or tree is "in" if its midpoint is <66 ft (20 m) from the centerline (tape).

7. Data entry

   a. Open the **Snag_Tutorial_Data.xls** file.

   b. Activate the **Data Entry** sheet.

   c. Click on **Move or Copy Sheet** under the **Edit** menu.

   d. Check the box **Create a copy**.

   e. Under **To book** click on (**new book**).

   f. Rename the new file, and then use this sheet to make hard copies for fieldwork.

8. To save the entered data as a CSV file:

   a. Activate the data entry sheet.

   b. Select **Save As** from the **File** menu.

   c. Scroll to find CSV (comma delimited) (*.**csv**).

   d. Click **Save**.

Appendix 2: Field Form Explanations

1. Stratum: Enter the stratum number: 1, 2, 3, or 4.

2. Location: Enter the polygon number or the geographic coordinates where the transect originates.

3. Transect: Assign a unique numeric identifier to indicate which 100-m or 400-ft transect length is being surveyed (for example, 1, 2, 3...). No two transects within a survey area should be the same number regardless of the stratum.

4. Subsegment: Assign a unique numeric identifier (1 through 8) to indicate which 12.5-m or 50-ft-long subsegment is being surveyed. The first subsegment of each transect should start with "1." This allows SnagPRO to join consecutive subsegments.

5. Distance: Enter the distance between the midpoint of the qualifying snag or tree and the center of the transect line to the nearest foot (nearest meter). If no snag is encountered within the entire subsegment, enter "9999" under distance. It is critical to measure distances accurately. If the midpoint of a snag or tree falls directly on the boundary, include the first one, exclude the second one, and so on. If a plot width has already been selected, enter "1" for distance.

6. Species: SnagPRO can accommodate either alpha (six characters) or numeric data. Listed below are the standardized numeric species codes taken from Stand Exam Program in the Pacific Northwest Region [USDA Forest Service 1991]. Customize for your own use:

Douglas-fir/redwoods:

Douglas-fir (*Pseudotsuga menziesii (*Mirb.) Franco)	202
Redwood (*Sequoia sempervirens* (D. Don) Endl.)	211

True firs:

Pacific silver fir (*Abies amabilis* Dougl. ex Forbes)	011
White fir (*Abies concolor* (Gord. & Glend.) Lindl. ex Hildebr.)	015
Grand fir (*Abies grandis* (Dougl. ex D. Don) Lindl.)	017
Subalpine fir (*Abies lasiocarpa* (Hook.) Nutt.)	019
California red fir (*Abies magnifica* A. Murray var. *magnifica*)	020
Shasta red fir (*Abies magnifica* A. Murray var. *shastensis* Lemmon)	021
Noble fir (*Abies procera* Rehd.)	022

Cedars:

Port-Orford-cedar (*Chamaecyparis lawsoniana* (A. Murr.) Parl.)	041
Alaska-cedar (*Chamaecyparis nootkatensis* (D. Don) Spach)	042
Incense-cedar (*Calocedrus decurrens* (Torr.) Florin)	081

Western redcedar (*Thuja plicata* Donn ex. D. Don)   242

Larch:
Western larch (*Larix occidentalis* Nutt.)   073

Spruce:
Brewer spruce (*Picea breweriana* Wats.)   092
Engelmann spruce (*Picea engelmannii* Parry ex Engelm.)   093
Sitka spruce (*Picea sitchensis* (Bong.) Carr.)   098

Pines:
Lodgepole pine (*Pinus contorta* Dougl ex. Loud)   108
Jeffrey pine (*Pinus jeffreyi* Grev. & Balf.)   116
Sugar pine (*Pinus lambertiana* Dougl.)   117
Western white pine (*Pinus monticola* Dougl. ex D. Don)   119
Ponderosa pine (*Pinus ponderosa* Dougl. ex Laws.)   122

Hemlock:
Western hemlock (*Tsuga heterophylla* (Raf.) Sarg.)   263
Mountain hemlock (*Tsuga mertensiana* (Bong.) Carr.)   264

Hardwoods:
Bigleaf maple (*Acer macrophyllum* Pursh)   312
Red alder (*Alnus rubra* Bong.)   351
Western paper birch (*Betula papyrifera* Marsh.)   376
Pacific madrone (*Arbutus menziesii* Pursh)   361
Golden chinkapin (*Castanopsis chrysophylla* (Dougl.) A. DC.)   431
Oregon ash (*Fraxinus latifolia* Benth.)   542
Tanoak (*Lithocarpus densiflorus* (Hook. & Arn.) Rehd.)   631
Quaking aspen (*Populus tremuloides* Michx.)   746
Black cottonwood (*Populus trichocarpa* Torr. & Gray)   747
Oregon white oak (*Quercus garryana* Dougl. ex Hook.)   815
California black oak (*Quercus kelloggii* Newb.)   818
Oregon myrtle (*Umbellularia californica* (Hook. & Arn.) Nutt.)   981

Other conifers:
Subalpine larch (*Larix lyallii* Parl.)   072
Cypress (*Cupressus* L.)   050

All junipers (*Juniperus* L.)	060
Pacific yew (*Taxus brevifolia* Nutt.)	231
Knobcone pine (*Pinus attenuata* Lemm.)	103
Limber pine (*Pinus flexilis* James)	113
Whitebark pine (*Pinus albicaulis* Engelm.)	101

7. Class: Enter the numeric code for the appropriate decay or structural class of the snag or tree encountered. Snag data should be collected on a data form separate from large trees. For snags, the numeric value should increase with increasing amounts of decay. For example, Parks and others (1997) have categorized snags into three structural classes.

    A. Snag classes

        1. Snags that have recently died.

        2. Snags that have been dead several years and have lost some branches and bark.

        3. Snags that have been dead more than several years and lack branches and bark (except grand fir and Douglas-fir, which tend to retain bark).

By contrast, numeric codes for the structural class of trees should decrease with increasing amounts of decay. For example:

    B. Tree classes

        1. Hollow

        2. Some decay evidence (broken branch or top, fungi, wildlife signs)

        3. Broomed trees

        4. Sound

Refer to Bull and others (1997) for detailed information on establishing categories and identifying trees useful to wildlife in the field.

8. D.B.H.: Enter the diameter at breast height of the snag or tree encountered measured with a d.b.h. stick or tape, to the nearest inch (cm).

9. Height: Enter the height of the snag or tree to the nearest foot (m).

10. Cavity: Enter the appropriate numeric code to indicate any nesting use of the snag or tree under consideration. In cases where it is not possible to determine whether any cavities are present, leave the Cavity field blank so that the snag is not included in the availability total.

    0. No cavities.

    1. New cavity indicated by one or all of following: fresh wood chips on ground below hole, light-colored wood around entrance, bird occupying cavity (excavated or natural).

    2. Old cavity: gray-colored chips on ground below hole, gray-colored wood around entrance, no sign of bird occupying cavity (excavated or natural).

    3. Both old and new cavities

    4. Other wildlife use.

11. Foraging: Enter the appropriate numeric code to indicate any foraging use of the snag or tree under consideration.

    1. New foraging indicated by light-colored wood around foraging sign, recent scaling.

    2. Old foraging indicated by gray-colored wood around foraging sign.

    3. Both old and new foraging.

    4. No foraging signs.

Appendix 3: General Computer Instructions for Snag or Large-Tree Analyses Within a Single Stratum

1. To get started:
   a. Double click on **SnagPRO.exe**.
   b. Click on **Snags or Trees** button under **Habitat Component**.
   c. From the **Measurement** menu, select **Metric** or **English**.
   d. Open your data file by clicking on **Open** under the **File** menu.
   e. Highlight the name of your comma-separated value (CSV) file and click **Open**.

2. To apply formula:
   a. Notice Segment and Section fields have been added and numbers computed for each column.
   b. Notice that four Width columns have been added.
   c. Click on **Multiple** tab in bottom left of screen for analyses with multiple species included; click **Single** for analysis of only one species.
   d. Enter minimum diameter at breast height in message box labeled "D.B.H."
   e. Enter minimum height of snags or trees to be considered in message box labeled "Height"; enter "0" if all heights will be considered or heights were not measured.
   f. Enter maximum value for decay or structural class in message box labeled "Decay Class."
   g. Enter numeric code of snag or tree species you would like to exclude (to include, if Single button was clicked) in box labeled "Species."
   h. From the **View** menu, decide upon a cost code for each stratum prior to initiating next section.

3. Summarize statistics:
   a. Click on **Optimal** tab at the top of the screen.
   b. Click on the first of the Optimal pages (**Optimal 1**).
   c. Check desired level of precision and t-value; if different values are desired, enter them and repeat steps 2c through 2g.
   d. Enter brief description of stratum and snag/tree characteristics for your records.
   e. In section labeled "Stratum to Process" highlight the **Single** circle.
   f. Click the **Compute** button.
   g. Examine Optimal pages for statistics, estimated sample size required, sample area required, lowest product and total cost values.
   h. Print copy of page if desired by selecting **Print Preview** from the **File** menu, then clicking tab labeled **Print**.

4. Conduct serial correlation test:
    a. Switch to Summary Statistics page.
    b. Click on **Correlation** button.
    c. Enter optimal transect length (section, segment, or subsegment) into "Correlation Length" input box.
    d. Enter optimal transect width into "Correlation Width" input box.
    e. Determine whether chosen plot size can be considered independent.

5. Density estimate:
    a. Click on **Densities** tab.
    b. Check to ensure t-value is correct for the analysis.
    c. Select **Simple-Random Sampling Equation** tab.
    d. Examine Densities sheet for estimated parameters and current level of precision to decide whether an adequate number of samples have been taken. Refer back to the Optimal page for additional number of samples needed to achieve desired level of precision.

6. Statistical test:
    a. Enter the target density into the "Target Value" box.
    b. Enter the estimated density into the "Estimated Value" box.
    c. Enter the bound of the estimated density.
    d. If target value (red line) falls within the bounds (green lines) of the estimated value (blue line), accept the null hypothesis that there is no difference between the estimated and target values for the given variable; otherwise, reject the null hypothesis.
    e. For borderline cases, consider additional sampling effort.

Appendix 4: General Computer Instructions for Snag or Large-Tree Analyses on a Stratified Landscape

1. To get started:
   a. Double click on **SnagPRO.exe**.
   b. Click on **Snags or Trees** button under **Habitat Component**.
   c. From the **Measurement** menu, select **Metric** or **English**.
   d. Open your data file by clicking on **Open** under the **File** menu.
   e. Highlight the name of your comma-separated value (CSV) file and click **Open**.
   f. Note that Segment and Section fields have been added and computed for each column.
   g. Note that four Width columns have been added.
2. To apply formula to all strata:
   a. Click on **Stratum 1** tab.
   b. Click on **Multiple** tab in bottom left of screen for analyses with multiple species; click **Single** for analysis of only one species.
   c. Enter minimum diameter at breast height in message box labeled "D.B.H."
   d. Enter minimum height of snags or trees to be considered in message box labeled "Height"; enter "0" if all heights will be considered or heights were not measured.
   e. Enter maximum value for decay or structural class in message box labeled "Decay Class."
   f. Enter numeric code of snag or tree species you would like to exclude (to include, if Single button was clicked) in box labeled "Species."
   g. From the **View** menu, decide upon a cost code for each stratum prior to initiating next section.
3. Summarize statistics:
   a. Click on **Optimal** tab at the top of the screen.
   b. Click on the first of the Optimal pages (**Optimal 1**).
   c. Check desired level of precision and t-value; if different values are desired, enter them and repeat steps 2b through 2f.
   d. Enter brief description of stratum and snag/tree characteristics for your records.
   e. In section labeled "Stratum to Process" highlight the **Stratum 1** circle.
   f. Click the **Compute** button.
   g. Enter a numeric value for total number of strata in this analysis in the "Number of Strata" input box.

    h. Enter one of six available cost codes into "General Cost per Sample" for the first stratum.

    i. Enter the area (in hectares or acres) of each of your strata.

    j. Examine Optimal pages for statistics, estimated sample size required, sample area required, lowest product and total cost values.

    k. Print copy of page if desired by selecting **Print Preview** from the **File** menu, then clicking **Print** tab.

4. Conduct serial correlation test:

    a. Switch to Summary Statistics page.

    b. Click on **Correlation** button.

    c. Enter optimal transect length (section, segment, or subsegment) into "Correlation Length" input box.

    d. Enter optimal transect width into "Correlation Width" input box.

    e. Determine whether chosen plot size can be considered independent.

    f. Repeat 3d through 3k and 4a through 4e for all strata.

5. Density estimate:

    a. Click on **Densities** tab.

    b. Check to ensure t-value is correct for the analysis.

    c. Select **Stratified-Random Sampling Equation** tab.

    d. Click **Calculate Stratified Values** button.

    e. Examine Densities sheet for estimated parameters and current level of precision to decide whether an adequate number of samples have been collected.

6. Sample size required:

    a. Click on **Sample Size** tab.

    b. Examine Optimal and Proportional sections for estimated sample sizes required within each stratum. Refer to the "Parameter Estimates for a Stratified Landscape" section on differences between two allocation methods.

7. Statistical test:

    a. Enter the target density into the "Target Value" box.

    b. Enter the estimated density into the "Estimated Value" box.

    c. Enter the bound of the estimated density.

    d. If target value (red line) falls within the bounds (green lines) of the estimated value (blue line), accept the null hypothesis that there is no difference between the estimated and target values for the given variable; otherwise, reject the null hypothesis.

    e. For borderline cases, consider additional sampling effort.

www.ingramcontent.com/pod-product-compliance
Lightning Source LLC
Chambersburg PA
CBHW080323290526
45790CB00005B/2158